Pandora's Box

Facing the shadow of the 8th house

Martin Sebastian Moritz

The Wessex Astrologer

Published in 2021 by
The Wessex Astrologer Ltd
PO Box 9307
Swanage
BH19 9BF

For a full list of our titles go to www.wessexastrologer.com

Originally published in German by Chiron Verlag as:
Das rätselhafte 8. Haus: Der Schatten im Horoskop

Cover design by Andy Jay

A catalogue record for this book is available at The British Library

ISBN 9781910531587

Contents

Chart Data

Adenauer, Konrad — 5 January 1876, 10:30 LMT, RR:AA, Cologne, Germany

Adler, Alfred — 7 February 1870, 14:00 LMT, RR:DD, Vienna, Austria

Ali, Muhammad — 17 January 1942, 18:35 CST, RR:AA, Louisville, Kentucky

Alice, Princess — 25 April, 1843, 04:05 LMT, RR:AA, London

Allen, Woody — 1 December 1935, 22:55 CST, RR:AA, New York

Antoinette, Marie — 2 November 1755, 19:30 LMT, RR:A, Vienna, Austria

Arendt, Hannah — 14 October, 1906, 21:15 MEH, RR:AA, Hannover, Germany

Beardsley, Aubrey — 21 August 1872, 17:18 GMT, RR:C, Brighton, England

Becker, Boris — 22 November 1967, 08:45 MET, RR:AA, Baden, Germany

Beckham, Victoria — 17 April 1974, 10:07 GDT, RR:DD, Harlow, England

Blair, Tony — 6 May 1953, 06:10 GDT, RR: AA, Edinburgh, Scotland

Bocuse, Paul — 11 February 1926, 16:00 GMT, RR:AA, Collonges-au-Mont-d'Or, France

Bogarde, Dirk — 28 March 1921, 08:30 GMT, Twickenham, England, RR:B

Bowie, David — 8 January 1947, 09:00 GMT, RR:A, London

Brennan, Chris — 1 November 1984, 13:28 MST, RR:AA, Aurora, Colorado

Caillebotte, Gustave — 19 August 1848, 15:20 LMT, RR:AA, Paris, France

Casiraghi, Pierre	5 September 1987, 02:46 MEDT, RR:A, Monte Carlo, Monaco
Castle, Barbara	6 October 1910, 14:30 GMT, RR:A, Chesterfield, England
Celestial: Neptune Discovery	24 September 1846, 00:00:15 LMT (= 12:00 AM) Berlin Obseratory, Germany
Corbyn, Jeremy	26 May 1949, 20:00 GDT, RR:C, Chippenham, England
De Mille, Cecil B.	12 August 1881, 05:14 LMT, RR:C, Ashfield, Massachusetts
Diana, Princess of Wales	1 July 1961, 19:45 GDT, RR:A, Sandringham, England
Edward VIII, King of England	23 June 1894, 21:55 GMT, RR:AA, Richmond, England
Ellis, Ruth	9 October 1926, 18:41 GMT, RR:C, Rhyl, Wales
Farage, Nigel	3 April 1964, 16:30 GDT, RR:A, Farnborough, England
Farrow, Ronan	19 December 1987, 10:49 EST, RR:A, New York
Ford, Betty	8 April 1918, 15:45 CWT, RR:AA, Chicago, Illinois
Galileo, Galilei	16 February 1564, Jul.Cal. (26 Feb 1564 Greg.) 15:41 LMT, RR:C Pisa, Italy
Garbo, Greta	18 September 1905, 19:30 MET, RR:AA, Stockholm, Sweden
George IV, King of England	12 August 1762, 19:24 LMT, RR:B, London, England
George, Prince of Cambridge	22 July 2013, 16:24 GDT, RR:AA, London
Gerber, Kaia	3 September 2001, 11:49 PDT, RR:AA, Los Angeles, California,
Hall, Judy	25 November 1943, 21:23 GDT, RR:A, Walsall, England
Henry VIII, King of England	28 June 1491 Jul.Cal. (7 July 1491 Greg.) 08:45 LMT, RR:AA, Greenwich, England
Hilton, Paris	17 February 1981, 02:30 EST, RR:C, New York

Hitler, Adolf	20 April 1889, 18:30 LMT, RR:AA, Braunau, Austria
Houdini, Harry	24 March 1874, 04:00 LMT, RR:B, Budapest, Hungary
Idemon, Richard	8 February 1938, 21:37 EST, RR:A Akron, Ohio
James, Jesse	5 September 1847, 00:00 LMT, RR:C, Kearney, Missouri
Johnson, Lyndon B.	27 August 1908, 05:40 CST, RR:C, Stonewall, Texas
Kennedy, John F.	29 May 1917, 15:00 EST, RR:A Brookline, Massachusetts
Kepler, Johannes	27 December 1571 Jul.Cal. (6 Jan 1572 Greg.) 14:37 LMT, RR:B, Weil der Stadt, Germany
Knievel, Evel	17 October 1938, 14:40 MST, RR:AA, Butte, Montana
Kurz, Sebastian	27 August 1986, 04:30 MEDT, RR:C, Wien, Austria
Leakey, Louis	7 August 1903, no time, Kabete, Kenya
Lenin, Vladimir	22 April 1870, 21:42 LMT, RR:DD, Simbirsk, Russian Federation
London, Jack	12 January 1876, 14:00 LMT, RR:B, San Francisco, California
Louis XV, King of France	15 February 1710, 08:18 LMT, RR:B, Versailles, France
Lugosi, Bela	20 October 1882, 15:30 LMT RR:A, Lugos, Romania
Luther, Martin	10 November 1483, Jul.Cal. (19 Nov 1483 Greg.), 22:46 LMT, RR:AA, Eisleben, Germany
Lynch, David	20 January 1946, 03:00 MST, RR:AA, Missoula, Montana
Macron, Brigitte	13 April 1953, 15:00 MET, RR: AA, Amiens, France
Madonna	16 August 1958, 07:05 EST, RR:DD, Bay City, Michigan

Mann, Thomas	6 June 1875, 10:15 LMT, RR:AA, Lübeck, Germany
March, Marion	10 February 1923, 03:46 MET, RR:A Nürnberg, Germany
Margaret, Princess	21 August 1930, 21:22 GDT, RR:AA, Glamis, Scotland
Marx, Karl	5 May 1818, 02:00 LMT, RR:AA, Trier, Germany
Mata Hari	7 August 1876, 13:00 LMT RR:AA, Leeuwarden, Netherlands
McQueen, Alexander	17 March 1969, 22:45 UT, RR:C, Lewisham, England
Melcher, Martin	1 August 1915, no time, North Adams, Massachusetts
Merkel, Angela	17 July 1954, 18:00 MET, RR:B, Hamburg, Germany
Monroe, Marilyn	1 June 1926, 09:30 PST, RR: AA, Los Angeles, California
Moore, Roger	14 October 1927, 00:45 GMT, RR:A, London, England
O'Neal, Ryan	20 April 1941, 09:34 PST, RR:AA, Los Angeles
Ocasio-Cortez, Alexandria	13 October 1989, 11:50 EDT, RR:A, Bronx, New York
Onassis, Jacqueline Kennedy	28 July 1929, 14:30 EDT, RR:A, Southampton, New York
Philip, Prince (Duke of Edinburgh)	10 June 1921, 10:00 EET, RR:AA, Mon Repos, Greece
Plath, Sylvia	27 October 1932, 14:10 EST, RR:A, Boston, Massachusetts
Pompadour, Madame de	29 December 1721, 10:15 LMT, Paris, RR:C
Renoir, Pierre Auguste	25 February 1841, 06:00 LMT, RR:AA, Limoges, France.
Richelieu, Cardinal	9 September 1585 (Greg.) at 09:28 LMT, RR:A Chinon, France
Sheen, Charlie	3 September 1965, 22:48 EDT, New York, RR:A

Spacey, Kevin	27 July 1959, 05:51 EDT, RR:X, South Orange, New Jersey
Stauffenberg, Claus von	15 November 1907, 01:00 MET, RR:AA Jettingen, Germany
Sutherland, Donald	17 July 1935, 11:30 ADT, RR:A, St John, New Brunswick
Talese, Gay	7 February 1932, 19:00 EST, RR:AA, Ocean City, New Jersey
Townsend, Peter	2 November 1914, 06:40 LST, RR:C, Rangoon, Burma
Ulbricht, Walter	30 June 1893, 13:20 MET, RR:AA, Leipzig, Germany
Van Gogh, Theo	1 May 1857, 03:30 MET, RR:A, Zundert, Netherlands
Verne, Jules	8 February 1828, 12:00 LMT, RR:AA, Nantes, France
Warner, Jack	2 August 1892, no time, London, Ontario
Westwood, Vivienne	8 April 1941, 01:00 GDT RR:C, Glossop, England

Foreword

Lynne Bell

A book like this, on the 8th house, has never been written before. And this befits a subject that is partially hidden from sight and surrounded by taboos. In the ancient world, many things could not be spoken of; they were mysteries hidden under the surface of acceptable discourse. Even now, mainstream culture, in different ways in different parts of the world, is often at odds with our private thoughts and actions, and our inner life is largely hidden from public view. Martin Sebastian Moritz has brought out some of these hidden experiences with great sensitivity and insight. He is both therapist and astrologer, and these dual professions have helped create a book of depth and insight into the complex psychological experiences that underlie human existence. For some, astrology is more event-oriented and descriptive; the astrology practised here takes in the living reality of the psyche. It examines how the unconscious forces of the 8th house shape our lives. For me it is essential reading.

Martin is unafraid of bringing light to the shadow places. He writes non-judgementally about a patient, Hannah, whose sexuality and drinking was often out of control, knowing this experience of illuminating the dark has great therapeutic value. The case studies of public figures are also fascinating and they touch on both the collective and individual impact of planets in these houses. Martin retells the stories of prominent public figures who had to hide "shameful" parts of themselves away: a withered arm, occult communication, homosexuality in 1950's Hollywood. Martin's examples reveal the many layers of experience and understanding required by any approach to the 8th house.

For some astrologers, only the written words of ancient astrology have weight. This approach forgets that not everything could be written, or even spoken out loud. Martin takes on material that is often unaddressed, or poorly understood by many astrologers. Over and over again he helps us to see how individuals deal with rejected parts of themselves. Some adaptations become monstrous, inimical to life, like Adolf Eichmann's cold extermination of the Jews in Nazi Germany. Martin takes a new look at some of the Nazi-era German charts, with its echoes for our own polarised time. Other examples show those who devour their own children out of emotional neediness, fuelled by the emptiness of profound loss. Some 8th house individuals, like Truman Capote, enter into deep intimacy with a subject, revealing their innermost thoughts, but perhaps also stealing something of another's pain and privacy for their own enrichment.

There is a moment when transits or progressions oblige us to look into the hidden aspects of our charts. Catching a glimpse of your own shadow side is breathtaking. It can pull you up short. Martin's section on natal placements and rulerships will bring you fully into the "terra obscura" of the 8th house. It can also begin the process of transforming the complexes that are found here, a process that is often long and hard to understand. I love the example of RuPaul's drag creativity as a way to activate the 8th house.

I am grateful to Martin for acknowledging my work on the 8th house, and moved that a lecture of mine on the Vampire was the spark for this excellent book. For any speaker, it's a rare privilege to know that your reflections, your words, have touched someone else's thinking, have influenced their practice. Reading Deborah Houlding's articles on the planetary joys, and then her landmark book, *The Houses: Temples of the Sky*, had a similar effect on my own thinking. While I had an immediate intuition that the material was important, it took quite a few years and much reflection for a new understanding of the houses to emerge. Martin explains those links I found between Hellenistic thinking and current practice, and how they illuminate a psychological approach to the houses.

My wish for you, as reader of this rich, thought-provoking book, is that you catch the spark from what Martin has written here, that you step into the sometimes dark passions of the 8th house with eyes wide open. With luck and persistance you may activate its power to leave behind an outgrown aspect of self. Things may die here, but they are also brought back to life in a new form.

10 August 2021

Lynn Bell

Villeneuve-sur Yonne, France

Preface

Vampires in the 8th house

I owe the very idea for this book to Lynn Bell. She gave a webinar on vampires and how we can be 'emptied out' by charismatic and seductive individuals. In it, Lynn talked about the sexually abusive and scandalous Lord Byron. He only used people for his own purposes without feeling any empathy whatsoever for his many victims, who fell for him. The reason for his vampiric nature was his upbringing. His father had only married his mother for her money and he spent it all, leaving her to fight for herself. His mother in turn clung to her only son in an emotionally abusive manner, leaving Byron basically viewing both men and women with suspicion; that if you want to survive in life, you'd better take advantage of others before they take advantage of you. Energy exchange is a core topic of the 8th house. And this energy can be in the form of sex, money and pretty much everything which has any value for the indvidual. As a matter of fact, it is impossible to live a life without entanglements, or without difficult circumstances which require a confrontation with our own shadow; another important aspect of the 8th house.

In her talk, Lynn also shed light on the Hellenistic approach to the 8th house, which was called *Epikataphora* (meaning 'to be cast down', which she further developed as the descent into the underworld.) It was feared as an evil, life-sucking 'empty place'. This linking of a Hellenistic overview with modern implications of psychological astrology helped me immeasurably in achieving a better understanding of this fascinating house. After all, my students and clients keep asking me about it, and yet never quite seem to be fully satisfied. And this is exactly how one should approach this mysterious house. The more you learn about it, the more you realise that certain aspects will always remain in the dark, in the shadow, in the unknown. And I am sure, that, although I tried to approach the research for this book from as many angles as possible, there will always be some hidden corner from which may come new insight...

Thank you, Lynn, for being such an inspiration.

Martin Sebastian Moritz
Berlin, Germany 2021

Introduction

The empty place

The psychological astrologer Karen Hamaker-Zondag calls the houses in the chart *circumstances*. This definition allows a broad range of interpretations, which is why I like the term. In Hellenistic astrology the 12 houses were called *places*. These places were calculated after the equal sign system. They had different levels of impact, depending on the kind of angle they formed with the ascendant, called *horoskopos*, which was the place of life energy.

The Greeks only allowed major aspects, because only those were believed to have a direct and thus energizing impact on the ascendant. The opposition angle (7th house) looks at the ascendant in a confrontational way, inviting a compromise. The sextile (3rd and 11th houses) is of a creative nature and thus has an encouraging effect. The trine (5th and 9th houses) has a benevolent and supportive effect. The square (4th and 10th houses) is challenging and requires self-reflection. The houses that only form minor aspects, which are semi-sextiles (2nd and 12th houses) and quincunxes (6th and 8th houses), on the other hand, were looked upon as maleficent by way of debilitating the native's life energy. These houses were feared as faulted; bad, foul or empty spaces. The 6th house, *kakos tyche* (*kakos* = bad, evil, *tyche* = goddess of fate, destiny), was a place of bad luck or illness. The 12th house, *kakos daimon* (*daimon* = spirit, in this case an evil and malevolent spirit) was particularly fearful. The polarity between the 2nd and the 8th house is rather fascinating. The 2nd house was called *anaphora* ('ascent from the underworld'), while the 8th house was called *epikataphora* ('descent into the underworld'). So both places were connected with the sinister underworld and thus, unsurprisingly, feared a great deal.

Like the other houses, which form only minor aspects with the ascendant, the 8th house was believed to be empty, thus not able to energize the ascendant. Or even worse, these houses were believed to literally suck out the native's energy, almost like parasites.

A tricky angle

If one considers the psychological impact of the tricky quincunx aspect, the notion of energy draining makes perfect sense. The 150° angle is a crooked angle. If someone looks at you from this angle it feels odd, because it doesn't allow you to face the other person directly. To be looked at from this 'crooked' position has a slightly irritating, unsettling touch to it. It feels unnatural and uncomfortable, often resulting in a constant underlying nervousness. The dynamics of this aspect are difficult to pin down. Since this position is so awkward, one wants to escape from it by turning the head slightly into the more natural and comfortable 180° position. It requires a great deal of flexibility to feel planets simultaneously which are in a quincunx relationship. They seem to work in an alternating light switch mode; each planet is either switched on or off. Whenever we shift our attention to one planet, the other feels automatically neglected and vice versa. This is why this aspect is also called *inconjunct*. It's like wanting to be in two places at the same time. This is a strain and it allows for very few moments of peace, which would occur only for short and precious moments. The dynamics of this angle can be both frustrating and stimulating. It often comes with a deep yearning to find peace and balance. It also holds true that the soul is never quite geared towards total stagnation. Instead it seems naturally given to constant shifting and movement, following the rules of daily karma.

Facing fearful odds

The 6th and the 8th houses both look at the ascendant from an awkward, inconvenient angle and challenge us to tackle tricky circumstances. This feels very burdensome, but it can also be the source of powerful transformation.

In order to be better able to confront these places and find out what they want from us, in a manner of speaking, we have to slightly readjust our thoughts. The 6th house deals with health and sickness, serving, and coping with everyday life. The 8th house is more complex. Amongst other issues, it deals with sexuality, temptation, self-conquest, psychology and spirituality, the values of others, debts, crime, taboos, crises, entanglements, death and transformation. Most of these issues, with the possible exception of sexuality, are disturbing, haunting and, to say the least, uncomfortable.

The 6th house constantly reminds us of the frailty of our health or how easily everyday life can plunge us into chaos. The 8th house goes even further and threatens us with severe crises and death. No wonder that this house was particularly daunting for the Greeks. As a matter of fact, even in modern times, this house hasn't lost much of its eeriness. Together with the 12th house, it is psychologically the most complex one. Students find it hard to grasp and clients fear it. And the reality, of course, is that we cannot escape it. And, at the end of the day, there is no growth or self-improvement without confronting our shadows and battling life's crises, often reflected by 8th house issues.

Projections

The 8th house is also a place where we like to project our longings and repressed passions onto other people. The German astrologer Wolfgang Doebereiner (1928 – 2014, Venus in 8th, Pluto rising) called this house 'Tendencies to fixation'. It means that the 8th house often represents our ideas of how things in life and other people ought to be. Since it encompasses the values of others and mutual values, it also represents everything which we long to have or, reciprocally, others want to have from us. Like looking behind a mirror we are, by interaction with others, confronted with our own issues.

Epikataphora: Descent into the underworld

The term *epikataphora* composes of *epi* = on, over, *kata* = down, *pherein* = to bring, transfer. It means descent into the world or casting down. The root word *kata* can also be found in *catastrophe* as well as in *catharsis*. It is in the underworld where we are confronted by our shadow, repressed soul issues and unfinished business; our dark side. This encounter often leads to the battlefields of a crisis. We are creatures of habit and want stability rather than change. And yet the old and obsolete has to die before something new can begin.

The ascendant is the place in the chart where the sun rises in the east. If we follow the movement of the sun on an idealised chart during the day, it reaches its zenith at noon at the Medium Coeli (MC). Afterwards the sun goes down and visits the 9th house and then, in the afternoon, the 8th. These hours are, in Mediterranean countries of hot summers, like Greece, the time of siesta. The sun now shines from an intensely bright, uncomfortably burning place. The 150° quincunx angle can feel almost blinding. To avoid this time of day, many people seek shelter in the shade and cool of indoors with windows shut and blinds pulled down or curtains closed. This natural rhythm can be found with many plants and animals. When the sun eventually visits the 7th house in the late afternoon it is cooler outside, and people come out again to socialise (cardinal air house). The 8th house, oddly enough, is the place of shadow during a time of day of very bright light. As Haruki Murakami puts it:

> "Where there is light, there must be shadow, where there is shadow there must be light. There is no shadow without light and no light without shadow...."

One could also say that the sun falls down from the zenith of the MC through the 9th, 8th and 7th houses. To fall has an interesting mythological connotation. Lucifer, a devil archetype, was originally an angel who fell from heaven and thus from God's grace to hell. A *fallen woman* was someone who has lost her innocence, meaning that she has surrendered her chastity and therefore must be punished by society by stigmatising and ostracising.

The 8th house is a symbol for a place where we can withdraw from the visible world in order to regenerate, before emerging to mix again with other people on a more superficial level in the 7th house. This seems to sound reassuring, but in reality it is not. Many of us shy away from the shadow and cool of self-reflection and much rather prefer the stimulation and diversion of the bright sunlight. To be 'on the dark side of life' is a metaphor for bad luck, despair and adversity. And still we all carry the seeds of the 8th house in us. They will always, when the time is ripe, come up to challenge us.

The 2nd house forms a semi-sextile with the ascendant and in Hellenistic astrology is called *anaphora* (*ana* = upwards, *pherein* = to bring, to transfer) = ascend from the underworld It is associated with the rise from the underworld. In Greece and Italy there are indeed places (caves etc.) which are believed to form actual entrance gates to the underworld. Astrologically we descend into the underworld in the 8th house and ascend from it in the 2nd house. This analogy can also be found in the course of the seasons. Each autumn (Scorpio time, 8th house analogy) nature seems to die. Each spring (Taurus time, 2nd house analogy) nature is reborn again.

Pandora's Box

In the myth, after Prometheus stole fire from the gods, Zeus, the king of gods, took revenge by presenting the beautiful Pandora to Prometheus' brother Epimetheus. She carried with her a mysterious box, which she was forbidden to open. But she was too curious to obey almighty Zeus and took a peek. This proved to be fatal. The box emptied its evil contents into the world. From that moment on the hitherto innocent world was exposed to vice, sickness and death. However, at the bottom of the box, there was one single precious thing left behind: hope.

This story exemplifies the main eight steps in and out of the core properties of the 8th house:

- Mystery
- Taboo
- Temptation
- Self-conquest
- Shadow
- Crisis
- Guilt
- Transformation

By looking for the deeply-buried truth of the 8th house we have to face our shadow. Without this we can never be whole. This confrontation is essential and absolutely necessary, so it requires a lot of courage. We simply need to bite the bullet, because this journey can never be easy. Whatever awaits us here, it is not nice, clean or pretty, but rather brings out traces of bitterness, shame or rancour. This might be a dirty, ugly side of us which we would normally try to suppress and hide both from the world and from ourselves. The smell which comes out of Pandora's Box is foul and yet enticing. These are the secret vaults of our subconscious. Before there is hope for the future, we must deal with unfinished business. It is at the very bottom of the box that the treasure lies.

Tendencies to fixation

I started my astrological studies at age 19 with Wolfgang Doebereiner's 'Munich Rhythm Method'. His definition of the 8th house, 'tendencies to fixation', has always mystified me. The 8th house encompasses in a way the ideas or view of the world to which we are attached or committed. This might include all kinds of ideals, systems and aberrations, but also all sorts of belief systems or cult figures upon which we might become fixated.

Scorpio is the sign of fixed feeling. We might become fixated on an idea to the extent that we feel that we own it (2nd house), we are possessed.

In the third quadrant is everything we encounter from outside. Everything we encounter is to a large extent the contents of our own imagination. The contents of the environment can only be decoded and used by the individual through images. We can put the receptivity to images in the 7th house, while the following 8th house encompasses our potential attachment to images and, in the final house in this quadrant, the 9th, lies the capacity to make use of these images. It is here that our inner capacity finds its object, materialisation and inspiration in the outside world. And so we also get in touch with our inner world and needs, symbolised in what we meet outside. This symbolism is the essence of what we encounter. We find inner archetypes in the things which have meaning for us, the magic complexity of wholeness in the things we encounter. We need constant input from other people and want to know whether we have made an impact on them. This can be enormously reassuring. The key trigger is to provoke a reaction in them, so that we in turn can feel something as well.

Only much later, when I started working as a psychodrama therapist, I began to grasp the dealings of the 8th house and how strongly they involve images. At first this definition comes across as rather abstract and vague, but if one gives it more thought, it actually does make perfect sense. The 8th house is indeed the place of attachment, as opposed to the 7th house, the place of encounters, which is more superficial and non-committal. The step from the 7th into the 8th house involves becoming more intimate and intense. When we attach ourselves to someone (or some idea or imagination), we have to give up a part of our own identity in favour of this relationship. We inevitably change. And often we have to deal with unexpected irritations, because things and people are seldom what we expect them to be. This is where the attachments enter into the wider picture. We all, consciously or unconsciously, have our attachments, (or 'images') and expectations, about how life in general and other people in particular ought to be. This may both apply for (overly) optimistic as well as (overly) pessimistic expectations. By linking these two terms, attachment and images, we may find ourselves entangled in these, our very own outer and inner worlds. Doebereiner wanted to find an umbrella under which all 8th experiences could be summarised. From my experience these images can often result in crises, which in turn again can lead to transformation, because life always forces us to challenge the way we deal with expectations, attachments and imaginations.

The 8th house holds a whole cornucopia of definitions in readiness. I was amazed by the overwhelming complexity during my research for this book. And if I compare my poor understanding on the 8th house from when I started so many years ago with what I know now about it, it is really mind-blowing. The final cherry on the cake was provided by American astrologer Lynn Bell in her lecture about vampirism and the 8th house, which was truly fascinating. It elaborates on the dynamics of energy exchange, seduction and dependency. So if you link everything together, you get the whole idea in a wider perspective and see the very essence. I wanted to write this book to dig up as many aspects about this fascinating place in the chart as possible, in order to offer greater clarity. So, let's not be lily-livered - let's fasten our seat belts for the bumpy journey into the underworld. And rest assured, as daunting as this journey might appear to you, at the end of the tunnel there will always be hope, just like at the very bottom of Pandora's Box.

Looking behind the mirror: The 2nd house
The flip side of the coin

The complex language of astrological symbols is one of polarity. It only makes sense if we put every component in relationship with its counterpart in order to get its full meaning. First of all, this applies to the heavenly bodies. The Sun should never be analysed without also taking its counterpart, the Moon, into account. If we look at Jupiter, Saturn must be considered as well. Secondly, this rule also applies to the houses in the chart. Their deeper psychological meaning becomes more vivid when they are linked with their responding opposite counterparts. It is a bit like looking at the flip side of the coin. A perfect example is transits and their journey through the houses. A transit always automatically influences the opposing house as well. If Saturn goes through the 10th house, it might indicate a time of tension in all career matters. At the same time the opposing 4th house will be affected likewise because we would need more support from our family, or face restrictions by not being able to rest and relax at home as much as we would have wanted to.

The polarity between the 2nd and 8th houses is particularly fascinating. We have already shed some light on this from the Hellenistic angle. And since that period this polarity has undergone some interesting changes in its meaning. The negative interpretations of the 'weak' Hellenistic 2nd, 6th, 8th and 12th places have, at least for one house, gained positive facets. While the 6th house is the house of illness and the 12th house a place of imprisonment, the 2nd house has mostly lost its negative connotation and become the house of all material and immaterial things of value; money, possessions and property. In modern psychological astrology this house is also associated with talents, self-worth and the ability to indulge. This almost makes this house-polarity a good cop, bad cop one.

Holding on or letting go

The 2nd house, in accordance with the Taurus sign, is all about building, collecting and holding on to material things. This is the place where we plant, collect and establish boundaries in order to feel reassured. A marked need for material reassurance in life becomes especially important when this house contains the ascendant ruler, the Sun, Mars or Saturn. Provided that there are no weakening aspects, these placements will probably favour some sort of material stability. The Moon, Uranus or Neptune in the 2nd, on the other hand, would rather indicate a fluctuation and constant uncertainty. Archetypal images for the 2nd house are soil, garden fence, larder, safety deposit box, bank safes, but also food-covered tables. Other definitions of the second house are:

- Resources, talents, my own values
- Boundaries of my own body, reassurance of everything material
- Pleasure and pain of my own body
- Mantra: I want everything to stay as it is now

If we look to the opposite side in the chart and look into the 8th house we find more complex archetypes:

- Hidden talents, inner resources
- My own values meet the values of others = everything is constantly changing
- Boundary crossings, the unknown behind material manifestations
- Pleasure and pain in (sexual) encounters with others
- Intimacy and intensity can be life-altering, so nothing stays the same
- The cistern, the pond, the compost heap

In our Western capitalist system money means power, status and security. The 8th house can be a collective area in our life rather than a personal one. At least that's how it feels most of the time. Values in the 8th house are controlled and influenced by the government, the state or the tax office, who decide how much we get to keep after they have taken their chunk. Only think of the drastic example of expropriations in the former German Democratic Republic after 1945. It is also no coincidence that the 8th house encompasses everything criminal. Stealing money, not declaring revenues or tricking others out of it can be punished, if found out.

To marry for love is a comparatively recent concept. For thousands of years it had been primarily a matter of security; pragmatic and unromantic. In the 8th house security means to seek contractual commitments, be it in marriage or business partnerships. Also borrowing money, investing in stocks and shares or coming into money by inheritance falls under the 8th house. Young George Byron, who grew up in poverty, inherits his uncle's money and title. This changes his life completely. Not only can he afford from then on to live a life of leisure, but also calls himself 'Lord Byron'. 'From rags to riches', as the phrase goes. Doris Day, on the other hand, faced bankruptcy after the sudden death of her husband and manager because he had wasted all her earnings and left her up to the ears in debt. The 8th house is about being possessed as opposed to having our own possessions in the 2nd house.

The values of others

The 2nd house defines our self-worth and self-esteem. It is here that we can find our talents, everything we own, and the sort of values that are important for us personally. To put it in a nutshell the formula can also be, 'Everything we can earn money from'. All three earth houses deal with earning a living (2nd), looking after ourselves (6th) and taking on responsibility (10th). Our awareness of what we are good at and what our talents are can influence our self-perception. If we look at the opposite house, the 8th, the whole concept of talents, possessions, and self-esteem gets turned upside down. Here everything gets defined by others. On a collective level we are influenced by society and our government, on a personal level by partners, our kin and peers. In the 2nd we find our own values, in the 8th it's the values of others. What is yours becomes mine and vice versa. We might contribute something to a partnership which will inevitably transform into something else. This counts not only on a material level, but on a psychological level as well. Every partnership transforms us. Committing oneself to a partnership requires letting go of our own values in order to create new, shared values. Look at Diana, Princess of Wales, with Moon and Jupiter in the 2nd house and Mars, Uranus and Pluto in the 8th. As a girl she used to romanticize about Prince Charles, who was her pin-up hero. She projected on him, the fairy tale prince, her inner need for security and love. But immediately after the wedding it hit her; the painful realisation that she was to be deeply disappointed. Little did she know that Charles' childhood had been every bit as emotionally cold as her own and that he was just as needy as her. Also, being suddenly thrust into the rigid rules of royal life and the dysfunctional patterns of her new family felt like hitting a wall. Her exposed, glamorous life in the spotlight came at an enormous cost. She felt manipulated, isolated and overwhelmed. Over the years she learned to use the press to her advantage and took revenge on Charles and the royal family, for which she was punished. The Queen stripped her of the title, 'Your Royal Highness', even though she was the mother of the future king of England. Diana's battle between her 2nd and 8th houses made her stronger and transformed her, but also showed her flaws and contradictions.

8th house crises, the descent into the underworld, often cause a transformation in our personality and a reassessment of values in our life. And while resources in the 2nd house are more obvious and easier to own, those in the 8th, strongly influenced by others and deeply challenging, may create new, hidden talents which make us stronger and more resilient.

Sexuality and transformation

The 2nd house rules our relationship with our own body. Do we feel comfortable with it? Does it bring us pleasure? Do we find ourselves at all attractive? Drag-artist RuPaul Charles says in his show, *RuPaul's Drag Race*, "If you can't love yourself, how the hell you gonna love somebody else?" Psychology acknowledges a form of narcissism which is called healthy narcissism, as opposed to toxic narcissism. It means that the individual is able to feel a mature form of positive self-esteem and self-confidence, while at the same time being able to feel genuine empathy for others.

The foundation of self-worth in the 2nd house can be challenged by all sorts of neurotic influences from the 8th, leading to painful self-questioning. The 8th house is the 2nd house of others. Do I expect my partner (7th and 8th) to pamper my own low self-esteem (2nd)? Do I want to live off his money and self-confidence? Or vice versa? Unrealistic expectations from partners, if unaddressed and unresolved, can often lead to fundamental crises which threaten the relationship. On the other hand, the intensive contact with a partner enables us to outgrow ourselves; the I and the You become an Us. But this requires a certain loss of control. The French call an orgasm *la petite mort*, the little death. Something dies, so that something else can be born. A powerful image for the 8th house.

1
Gateway to Another World

Souls never die, but always on quitting one abode pass to another. All things change, nothing perishes. The soul passes hither and thither, occupying now this body, now that...So, the Soul being always the same, yet wears at different times different forms.
Pythagoras

The soul is everlasting, and its learning experience is lifetime after lifetime.
Shirley MacLaine (Sun, Mars and Uranus in the 8th house)

Spiritualism is a religious movement based on the belief that the spirits of the dead exist and have both the ability and the inclination to communicate with the living. The afterlife, or the "spirit world", is seen by spiritualists, not as a static place, but as one in which spirits continue to evolve.
Wikipedia

What happens after death?

This is a question which we inevitably have to ask ourselves if we enter the 8th house. Do you believe in life after death? Is it only the body which dies, but not the soul? Where does the soul go? To heaven? To hell? Is there something like Nirvana? Or does the soul get stuck in a sort of intermediate realm, able to get in contact with those who are still alive?

Planets in the 8th house might indicate our individual image of death. Venus might indicate a peaceful, easy death. Saturn can stand for a more melancholy and grave idea of what death means.

Where the sun doesn't shine...

The ancient Greeks regarded the 8th house as the entrance into the underworld, where the demons lived. All souls have to pass through this gateway in their dying moment. This realm is one of shadows, where the sun doesn't shine. This is odd insofar as during the daily journey of the Sun through the houses, the early afternoon hours are particularly hot with the Sun being at her most stinging, glistening brightness. In Mediterranean countries everything shuts down during this hour, called *siesta*. People retire into the cool and dark of their homes and yards and close the shutters. Noel Coward famously said: "Only mad dogs and Englishmen go out in the midday sun." In ancient Egypt people imagined that the Sun god Ra, after disappearing from the horizon after dark, would travel through the scary realm of the dead during the night to transform himself, before remerging again in the morning. The symbol for this mystical phenomenon is the shiny black scarab beetle, which rolls dung into a ball as food and as a food chamber in which to lay eggs; this way as the larvae hatch they are immediately surrounded by food. This captures most vividly the heavenly cycle and the idea of rebirth or regeneration.

Loss and mourning

> *I have lost a treasure, such a sister, such a friend as never can have been surpassed. She was the sun of my life, the gilder of every pleasure, the soother of every sorrow.*
> Cassandra Austen after the death of her companion and sister, Jane Austen, at age 41, in 1817.

When a beloved one dies it's like the sun has ceased to shine. Death leaves a hole in our lives; we shiver in the cold nothingness and loneliness. Most people have considerable difficulties with accepting death because they don't want to face the painful feelings which are involved. They find it hard to let go, as the death often leaves behind too many questions and unresolved feelings. Many may find comfort and hope in the perception that death indeed is not the final end, but that there will eventually be a reunion with the loved one.

Death cult

The Victorian era was the heyday of obsession with the realm of death. This was a time of fast changes in the form of growing capitalism, inhuman industrialisation and scientific proof that God didn't create the world after all. Charles Darwin claimed that the human race descended from the ape, and religion fell more and more out of fashion for the intellectually enlightened elite. On the other hand, exchanging a worldview which revolved around God with one which was rationally based on science and biology left many feel unsatisfied and desperate. They experienced a crisis of faith and longed for spiritual reassurance and comfort. If there was no higher force like a god who created man, wouldn't it logically follow that there wasn't such a thing like an immortal soul either? And that there wasn't an afterlife at all?

The counter-reaction to this rational trend was the growing fascination with the 'shadow world', also called spiritualism. Artists responded with the Romantic movement, which involved the fascination with long since gone ancient periods of history. They found inspiration and refuge in classic Greece and the Middle Ages. This setting was the perfect background for a transfigured, sentimental world of ghosts, fairies, heroes and damsels in distress, like in the mythical realm of Avalon, where King Arthur and the Knights of the Round Table were looking for the Holy Grail.

The 19th century was also extreme in other aspects. Not only on account of the dramatically fast progress of industrialisation, but also because of new forms of deadly threats in the form of plagues like smallpox, typhus, yellow fever and cholera; famines, like the one caused by potato blight in Ireland, forced millions to emigrate. Also, mass warfare in the Crimean war (1853 – 1856) was introduced, which led to the foundation of modern nursing and later the establishment of the Red Cross. Other wars in the 1860s and 1870s saw mass killings and left millions of parents, spouses and siblings bereft and in dire need of consolation. Spiritual seances with mediums, which tried to establish contact with the deceased by way of channelling, séance tables, trances or Ouija, became popular.

By the mid-19th century churchyards were too crowded to serve any longer as burial sites, so many European capitals such as London and Paris began to build a new kind of cemetery, on a scale larger than ever seen before. Just think of Père Lachaise in Paris and Highgate in London. These are huge, monumental cities of the dead, with their melancholy marble angels, dramatic mausoleums and highly sophisticated use of classic architecture on many gravestones, to reflect a deep need to honour the dead and have a place where one can go to remember them. Obviously, these grounds were expensive and only affordable to the aristocracy and the very rich new social class of upscale bourgeoisie. When poor people died, they often ended up on the dissection table for medical experiments.

Old cemeteries have always been immensely popular on account on their morbid and melancholy atmosphere, weather-worn patina and faded inscriptions. In Latin America people gather in cemeteries on *el dia de los muertos* (the Day of the Dead) to celebrate with the whole family in a day of joy; eating, drinking, and playing music to remember the deceased. They pretend, or actually believe, that the deceased, on this special day, really are with their living descendants.

The Widow of Windsor

The most famous person of the Victorian age was the Queen herself. Victoria (1819 – 1901) had 5 planets in the 12th house and Neptune in the 8th, as lord of the 11th house (society), in which Pisces is intercepted. She ruled the British Empire, on which the sun never set. Destiny hit her particularly hard. When her beloved husband and companion, Prince

Albert, suddenly died in 1861, the 42-year-old monarch and mother of nine was shattered. Inconsolably grief-stricken, she sank into a deep depression and developed an unhealthy fixation with her dead husband in the form of a morbid death cult. His room was to be preserved in exactly the state in which he had left it. She regularly consulted his marble bust. Laughing, cheerfulness, having any kind of fun was strictly prohibited at court and within her family circle. For the rest of her life, another 40 years, she remained the 'widow of Windsor', dressed in black. This neurotic stubbornness, one of her most marked characteristics, had a fatal influence on her children. Her youngest, Beatrice, who was only four years old at the death of her father, served the Queen as a sort of perverted mourning toy. She clung desperately to the helpless child, and nobody dared to intervene. Any sign of growing up and seeking independence in Beatrice, called 'Baby', was vehemently suppressed by the needy mother. The result was a premature ageing in the young woman, who had to serve as a kind of ersatz partner. In photographs Beatrice looks like an old woman, a sign of vampirical maternal energy draining dry her vitality. She was allowed to marry, however, but only under the condition that her husband, a distant and poor relative, would also live under the same roof, financially dependent upon and psychologically manipulated by Victoria.

The path through the gate

There are many ways to get in contact with 'the other world'. A Greek myth, however, claims that we have to use a ferryman who will convey us safely over the river Styx to the other shore. This magical figure, Charon, has to be paid a fee, he won't do it just as a favour. This is the reason why, in so many ancient cultures, the dead were buried with a coin placed on their closed eyelids or between their lips. If the soul is left without this coin it can never be delivered safely to the underworld, but will be destined to wander forever in a sort of intermediate realm between life and death, unable to rest in peace. No wonder the ancient Greeks feared the 8th house. So not only do we have to travel to the spooky underworld after our death, we also have to pay for it. This takes care of two of the most important facets of this house; letting go and being in debt.

Using a medium to get into contact with any sort of 'other world' also requires a certain willingness to 'let go' (of scepticism etc.) and, although some spiritual mediums don't charge, having to pay for it. Whether these sorts of contacts are fruitful or comforting of course depends on many different aspects, and I myself am the last person to pass judgement here. Suffice to say, I have also tried my hand at the odd Ouija session and reincarnation hypnosis as well. With mixed results...

Good and evil spirits

What are our deepest motivations in seeking contact with this other world? And what motivates the 'ferryman' or 'medium'? Do we simply want a little tickle, to seek answers or comfort? Do we realise how vulnerable we are in doing this? And what kind of power do we attach to these sorts of spiritual beings? Do we believe them to be all good? Or are there also evil beings who can harm us? Do we believe in angels, in devils and evil demons? All these questions have to be dealt with, because we could subconsciously project our own hopes and fears onto these creatures. Opening Pandora's Box can be dangerous...

The concept of reincarnation

The 9th house is the house of religion and faith. What is our particular purpose in this life? Do you believe in any kind of divine power? Do you find solace by belonging to a certain religion? In the previous 8th house, you have to ask yourself another question, which is crucially linked with faith, or the lack thereof. The 8th house encompasses death and reincarnation. So, before you enter the 9th house, you have to spend some time in the

8th, contemplating on how you stand on life after death. Do you believe in the rules of karma and reincarnation? Will our souls be reborn into a new body? Do we already know the people in our close circle from other incarnations? Is what we experience and attract in this life the result of previous ones? Or is our life here on earth merely a colossal cosmic joke with no purpose whatsoever? This is heavy stuff, I know. But doesn't believing in reincarnation widen our range for interpretation enormously? In karmic astrology the 4th, 8th and 12th houses, along with retrograde planets and the nodes, play an important role.

The following examples demonstrate how becoming entangled with 'the other world' can seriously affect the lives of people, either in a positive or a negative way.

Conversations with Angels

London, 1581. John Dee, the well-known astrologer, astronomer, mathematician, navigator and mystic, has reached a turning point in his life. At age 54, the scientist, whose most marked characteristics are, besides his genius, an insatiable curiosity for everything mysterious and unfathomable, can look back on a rich and impressive life. He had been educated at the most renowned European universities. Over the years, he had met and measured himself up against the great minds of his time. Dee had been a friend of the great astrologer Tycho Brahe and was familiar with Copernicus' work. Queen Elizabeth herself holds him in high esteem, which has opened many doors for him.

But yet, he feels deeply frustrated. After all, he still hasn't found the answers to his most pressing questions. These questions revolve around the essence of life and the overarching secrets of the universe. And still, there must be something out there which is deeper, more all-encompassing and truer than anything being taught at universities; something fundamental, another hidden truth behind the obvious, material truth. Something

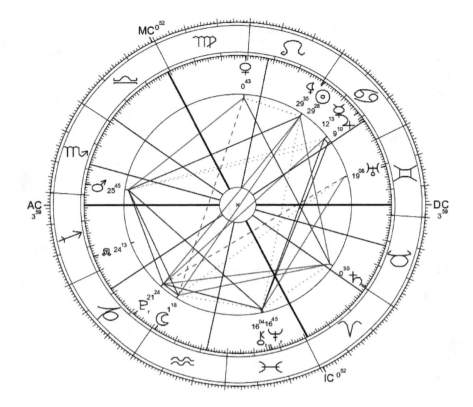

John Dee, 23 June 1527 Gregorian, 16:02 LMT, London, RR:DD

8th house constellations

- Sun, Mercury, Jupiter and Black Moon Lilith in 8th
- Saturn as apex of T-square with Sun in 8th and Moon (ruler of the 8th) in 2nd
- Sun, ruler of 9th, Mercury ruler of 7th and 9th (Virgo intercepted), Jupiter ruler of 1st
- Sun trine Mars in Scorpio in 12th
- Pluto as ruler of 12th in 2nd, trine Mars and Neptune

spectacular and yet simple. The renaissance period is a age of contradictions. On the one hand science has made vast improvements in many areas and people know more and more about the material world. It is the age of discovery and conquests. On the other hand, many people still believe in fairies, ghosts, demons and angels. The Catholic church, passionately committed in its revengeful counter-reformation movement, tries to wipe out all sorts of superstition by implementing the powerful weapon of the Inquisition. England, however, remains staunchly protestant. The Queen, although being forced to suppress Catholicism, is tolerant, and doesn't 'have any desire to make windows into men's souls.' She, like many other monarchs of the time, seeks astrological advice and even has her coronation date selected by John Dee.

The fatal look into the crystal ball

A year ago, while studying old manuscripts, Dee had come across fascinating traces of an ancient occult language, called Henochian. In the Hebrew bible Henoch is the son of Jared and father of Methuselah, not to be confused with Cain's son Enoch.

According to the Apocryphal books he was directly taken up to heaven by God himself and made guardian of the archangels and all the celestial treasures, being privy to all mysteries. Some sources even identify him with the Metatron, the angel who communicated God's word.

The interest in angels is also popular among other scientists. Some refer to them as their 'guardian angels', certain that learning their language would hold the key to obtaining all answers. From now on Dee is obsessed with learning this mystical language, which will enable him to communicate with the heavenly creatures. He has already experimented with several spiritual mediums, but without any satisfactory results. Then he is introduced to the incredible Edward Kelley. Young Kelley's reputation, however, is not unblemished. While some testify that he is a genuine medium, others put him down as a fraud. He has already come into contact with the law on account of document forgery. Dee blows concern to the wind and puts Kelley to the test. The two hit it off instantly, the beginning of an almost symbiotic cooperation which will last for six years. The set-up for their seances never alters. After looking into a crystal ball for a certain period, Kelly sinks into a deep trance. The ball is always positioned on a special table, surrounded by symbols, a hexagram and a key to decipher the transmitted letters and words. Then the ball releases a light which takes possession of Kelley and enables him to channel messages from the other side. Strange ghostly entities come through; delicate, fairy-like, coquettish. At other times other creatures show up; less fragile and seductive, but rather frightening and monstrous, resembling more demons than angels.

At first the seances are aiming to decode the key to the Henochian language. Later the angels are asked to explain the complexities of the universe. More and more entities show up, their angelic ranks in strict hierarchical order. They give away all sorts of details on the role of the four elements and nature and instruct Kelley and Dee to recite specific spells.

They penetrate deeper and deeper into the subject, in the end even daring to unravel the secret of the philosopher's stone; the mythical formula to manufacture gold. This would indeed mean putting them into a position of unlimited power. John Dee's diaries suggest that the two are at some point so consumed in their contacts with these strange creatures that they are on the brink of exhaustion, if not madness.

By and by word gets around about the strange goings on. More and more people become curious. When a Catholic aristocrat from Eastern Europe visits and wants to witness their experiments, it alerts the Queen's secret service. They suspect black magic or dealings with a foreign power, which would be treason. To escape arrest, torture and the death penalty they have to escape to the continent. They zigzag all across Europe, in search of a secure hideout. Eventually they find shelter at the legendary court of eccentric emperor Rudolf II in Prague, who is fascinated by alchemy and magic. The seances become more and more extreme and debilitating, and the increased frequency seems to attract different kinds of apparitions. The formerly fragile and gentle angels make way for a provocatively naked and seductive siren, who tries to get the two men under her spell.

Final crisis and end

In order to transmit further messages, the siren demands that the men switch wives in order to commit adultery. We don't know whether they actually obeyed this. All we know is that shortly after this it comes to the final rift and separation. Kelley tries his hand at working as an alchemist on his own and finds an aristocratic sponsor. The latter, however, has him arrested after he fails to actually manufacture gold. Kelley is killed while trying to escape.

Dee returns to England, where he is in for a big shock. His library, which once had been the most precious in the country, has been badly ransacked. Only shreds of single books remain; the scavengers have done a good job. Moreover, he has lost his influence at court. The old Queen Elizabeth had lost interest in his work during her final years, but her successor, the pious and superstitious James I, is a totally different matter. Under his reign astrologers are being pursued as heretic sorcerers and severely punished. During his last years, Dee again and again tries to contact the angel beings, but all in vain. He dies poor and forgotten at age 80. His legacy, however, lives on under his followers who value his work about navigation, astrology and the Henochian communications.

In the film *Elizabeth, The Golden Age*, John Dee tells the Queen:

> "This much I know...When the storm breaks, each man acts in accordance with his own nature. Some are dumb with terror. Some flee... some hide... And some spread their wings like eagles and soar on the wind."

The fixed T-square: A tenacious powerhouse

Sun conjunct Lilith in the 8th house as part of a T-square with the Moon and Saturn stands for a quest for answers from deep within. Lilith always says no to conventional ways of behaviour and moral values. She has to follow her own, unorthodox ways. In the 8th house she has to break taboos to free herself. In Dee's chart she also embodies the fixation with the female angelic/demonic spirits, who show themselves by way of conjuring in the seances. Saturn in Taurus in the 5th house sits on the apex of the T-square and revels in material manifestations, since this is a very earthy combination. Everything which has to do with sensuous nature and measurable dimensions becomes the pivotal point of self-expression (5th house), but can also easily become a fixed idea. Saturn in Taurus is particularly obstinate, processing experiences rather slowly and needing constant repetition. Like a dog with a bone, John Dee just wouldn't give up on his quest, even if he needed hundreds, or thousands of seances. Also the Moon in the 2nd house takes part in the T-square. In Aquarius, this Moon normally comes with a tendency to split overwhelming feelings and rather drift off to mental spheres. Since the Moon rules the 8th house, it is vital to import the values of others (8th) into one's own values (2nd). The beneficial aspects of both luminaries, and Mars in Scorpio in the 12th house, makes the native aware that there are powerful dealings going on behind the scenes so maybe they will have answers ready as events unfold. Mars, the classical ruler of the 12th stays right there, almost stuck. The modern ruler, Pluto, on the other hand, is in the 2nd house, indicating that something transient and dreamlike (12th) should become something solid (2nd). Mars in Scorpio is in his domicile and thus particularly resilient, albeit his motives remain somewhat hidden and hard to grasp (12th).

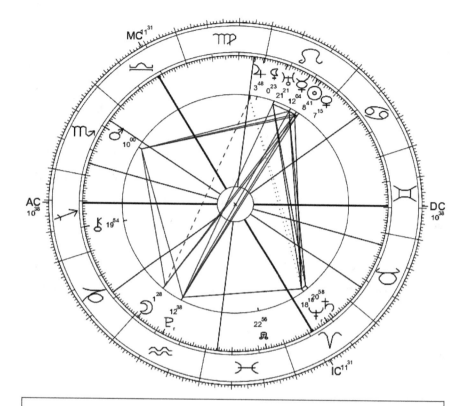

Composite John Dee/Edward Kelley
Edward Kelley 1 August 1555 Julian (11 August 1555 Greg.) 16:05 LMT,
Worcester, England, RR:A

8th house constellations

- 5 placements in 8th: Sun, Mercury, Venus, Jupiter and Black
  Moon Lilith
- Moon conjunct Saturn and Neptune at IC, with Moon as lord of
  the 8th
- Stellium in 8th as base of kite with Pluto at the tip
- Stellium & Pluto as parts of T-square with Mars in Scorpio as
  apex in 11th

A Plutonian kite

Planets which assemble in a stellium always experience a kind of energy boost and a highly charged interaction. None of the participants can function on its own, uninfluenced by its neighbours. The native will often feel self-involved and conflicted. This holds particularly true if one the luminaries are affected. The stellium in this composite is a veritable powerhouse, most of its planets are in Leo in the 8th house. The chart has a lot of fire, which perfectly indicates the passion which both Dee and Kelley approach their quest. After all, to tirelessly undertake countless seances requires great conviction. Incidentally, Kelley's chart also displays the Sun in the 8th house.

Let's have a closer look at this planetary accumulation in the house of Pandora's Box. Unsurprisingly, this partnership ticks almost every box of 8th house manifestations. Firstly, it fits with the 'gateway to the underworld'. Time and again they try to stay in contact with the spirits. Secondly it is in line with 'tendencies to fixation'. They believed right until the end that it was actually there, in the ghostly parallel world, where all the answers to their urgent questions lay. Furthermore, they find themselves deeply involved with the 'values of others', both in a material way (manufacturing gold), as well as in a spiritual way (were their seances witchcraft or not?). Another correlation is 'criminal acts and danger'. More than once they come into conflict with the hand of justice and risk their lives. Also, 'sex and seduction' are involved, as well as 'breach of taboo'; a female ghost encourages adultery. And finally, we hit 'crisis and transformation'. Many times they are at the very brink of total disaster. Not only do they endanger their lives and mental health, but also their immortal souls, because they commit a sin. The answer to the question of whether or not this cooperation transformed their lives seems pretty obvious. Their lives changed dramatically, and after splitting up, both men found that they couldn't return to the lives they led before.

Pluto sits at the tip of the kite in the 2nd house. The fact that their path is so burdensome can be explained by Pluto partaking in a T-square with Mars in Scorpio in the 11th house (society). Since there are too many interested parties (11th) involved who all want something different, there is no real chance of success. What's more, the challenging placement of Saturn and Neptune at the IC indicates the impossibility of bringing contradictory energies together. The IC stands for the roots. Neptune suggests a tendency to become disillusioned and it rules all dissolving and rotting processes. Saturn, on the other hand, wants to give something a solid form. In Aries this planet is having a hard time, since patience is anathema to this quick and feisty sign. So, what's left? The North Node is in Pisces in the 3rd house, which stands for dealing with information (3rd) about all things spiritual, dreamy, illusional and transient (Pisces).

Expert on Dying: Elisabeth Kübler-Ross

I know beyond a shadow of a doubt that there is no death the way we understood it. The body dies, but not the soul.
Elisabeth Kübler-Ross

Dying as a taboo

Billings hospital, Chicago, 1965. The 40-year-old, Swiss-born doctor, Elisabeth Kübler-Ross, takes up her new position as assistant professor for psychiatry. After the birth of her second child, she is very eager to work again. This birth, like the first one, has been emotionally unsettling. She had lived through several miscarriages and experienced painful episodes of intense mourning and post-natal depression. Even at a very young age, she had been confronted with bereavement in her family. Her whole life, it seems, has been a battle of life and death. As the first born of triplets, her own survival had been almost a miracle, because she was much too small and weak, but her loving and devoted mother nursed her through, so that little Elisabeth was able to survive.

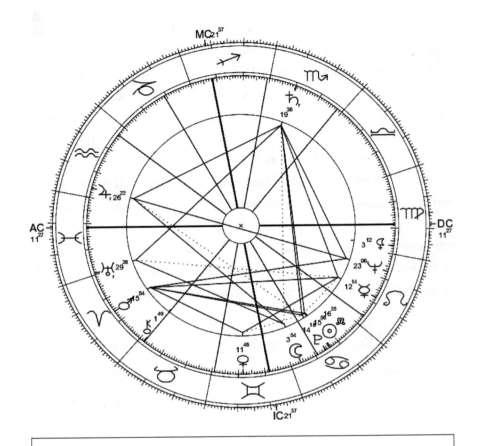

Elisabeth Kübler-Ross, 8 July 1926, 22:45 MET, Zurich, Switzerland, RR:A

8th house constellations

- Saturn retrograde in Scorpio in 8th as ruler of 11th (modern) and 12th (traditional)
- Saturn as apex of T-square with Jupiter retrograde in 12th and Neptune in 6th
- Pluto as ruler of 8th in 5th, conjunct Sun and North Node
- Sun/Pluto square Mars in 1st

The relationship with her father, however, has been less loving. He refuses to give the bright and ambitious girl a higher education, simply on account of her sex. But, being a true fighter, she runs away from home and struggles alone, finally even realising her big dream to become a doctor. She falls in love with an American, marries him and they settle in Chicago.

Her new post, instead of making her happy, has the quite opposite effect. She is shocked and frustrated by the way the overworked staff treat the terminally ill patients. Nobody is trained to deal with dying people, nor is there even enough time. This is a dilemma. After all, a hospital is supposed to heal its patients, not let them die. But what happens with patients who are diagnosed with a fatal, incurable illness? Since there is no way to improve their medical condition, they are left to themselves, with their helplessness, fear and desperation. If they are lucky, they have relatives and friends who come to visit, or maybe a priest will convey comfort. But far too many are just alone in the world. This careless dealing with the dying is a symptom of the spiritual vacuum in modern western society. By 1965, the Christian faith of charity and the comforting belief in a better life after death has become obsolete and out of touch with life in a pragmatic capitalist society. And why should this attitude be any different in a hospital? The staff feel uncomfortable and ill-prepared with this issue and avoid contact as much as possible. After all, there is no such thing as psychological training, no time for listening or giving comfort.

Doctor Kübler-Ross, however, is not willing to accept this. She wants to help these patients and refuses to fall into the routine of simply ignoring the problem. So she sets up a plan to spend as much time as she can with them, on top of her regular working hours, and unsalaried. Listening to them is the most important part. Thankful for the attention, they share their feelings with her. And naturally, they also talk about death and dying, which for most people is very uncomfortable - but not for Kübler-Ross. She wants to know all about it. She is intrigued. What ideas do the patients have about death and a possible afterlife?

The usually neglected patients are, of course, very appreciative. And what they have to say, Kübler-Ross realises, bears a veritable treasure of astonishing insights. She starts to record and transcribe everything. She feels that this is not merely a personal need anymore, but rather a groundbreaking project which could have implications both for other experts as well as for affected relatives. *On Death and Dying* is published in 1969. The book is met with great interest and still forms the foundations of modern palliative care. Particularly helpful, even today, is her model of the five stages of grief. They describe the process which anyone who is terminally ill, including their relatives and friends, can use to deal with any kind of 'unfinished business'. Furthermore, they can not only be applied to the actual process of dying, but to all sorts of severe sufferings from loss, like divorce or losing a job.

These five stages are:

1. **Denial**: The diagnosis is refused, the dying denies the unavoidable out of self-protection.
2. **Anger**: The dying is envious of everyone who is not terminally ill and allowed to live on, and lets out their anger on them.
3. **Bargaining**: The dying tries, via remorse, to bargain with God, to ease the pain, to prolong life, etc.
4. **Depression**: The feeling of desperation and the growing awareness that life will go on without them is an important phase of grief and requires a lot of patience from everyone concerned
5. **Acceptance**: The dying gives up fighting and prepares for imminent death. For relatives and friends it is now equally important to comply so that the patient doesn't have to feel guilty. This is also the final opportunity to resolve unfinished business.

The ultimate taboo: Near-death experience

Kübler-Ross adds further publications to this newly-created area of research into death and dying. By now she is a recognised authority and held in high esteem all over the world; she gives lectures, takes part in discussions on TV shows and receives various awards. But despite her success she doesn't feel quite satisfied. She feels she must keep on digging even deeper. There are cases where patients talk about experiences which don't really fit with conventional perceptions of death and dying. It is the elephant in the room, the highly controversial phenomenon of near-death experiences.

Her method stays the same: interviews with hospital patients. She analyses over 20,000 cases, who all claim to have been clinically dead and, eventually, brought back to life. The astonishing fact, she concludes, which is of course scientifically refutable, must be that there isn't such a thing as actual death.

The soul leaves the body

Many describe their near-death experience as liberation, and compare physical death with a butterfly leaving the cocoon, or like simply moving out of one house into another. The participants describe the unique sensation of being able to observe their own body from above. They often remember every little detail, such as people present at the scene, the colour of a dress, or what someone said, thought or felt. The whole experience is often described as 'feeling whole again'.

Distance in time and space don't matter anymore. A dead person would be able to travel thousands of miles to give a loved one a sign and say goodbye. After this, passing over to the other world is compared with crossing a tunnel, a bridge or a mountain pass. The eternal soul, clinging to a sort of silver umbilical cord, is finally cut, but only after the actual death of the physical body. At the end of the tunnel there would be a light, which radiates a hitherto unknown, infinite peace. Simultaneously, the dying experiences a kind of flashback. Every past moment in their life flashes back into conscience with all its karmic implications. After realising that the final moment of goodbye has not yet arrived after all, and the body is restored to life, the near-death experience has an enormous after-effect. Nearly all participants state that they have lost their fear of death. Dying patients can sometimes regress and become small children again. They can get in touch again with their invisible playmates, whose existence in their childhood was always denied by parents and other adults. For Kübler-Ross, these creatures are spirits that surround all of us, even though we're not aware of them.

Concerned family members and colleagues warn her against sharing her results with a broader audience, but she throws caution to the wind. And indeed, the publication is a huge scandal and she loses all credibility with most of her colleagues. Many even distance themselves from her for good. The following years are very difficult and lonely. Within a short period of time, both of her houses are burnt down to the ground, along with all her transcripts and valuables. She suffers several strokes and ends up in a wheelchair. But she just won't budge and perseveres in her studies. Aged 78, she dies peacefully, surrounded by relatives and friends, eager to go into the light.

The chart: Saturnian resilience

The chart clearly indicates her determination and willingness to fight. Mars in Aries in the 1st house in a square with Sun/Pluto in the 4th house gives tenacity and defies anyone who claims that the native might be a quitter. This is the stuff of which true inner resilience is made. The T-square in fixed modality also supplies great inner strength. Saturn in Scorpio as apex in the 8th house is the astrological equivalent to the last man standing on the battlefield. Saturn rules the 11th, the house of groups, like-minded people and of social developments. Additionally, he rules the 12th house (traditional ruler of Aquarius); the house of dissolution, unconsciousness and mystery. Kübler-Ross' motivation is to take on responsibility (Saturn), for a specific group (terminally ill patients, people with near-death experience), by breaking taboos and transforming attitudes about death (8th house). She succeeds by spending time with the afflicted and letting them tell her everything about their dreams, fears and images about another world, after death (12th house). She forces (Saturn in Scorpio), society (11th house), to look into the abyss (8th house). This requires a lot of self-sufficiency, because her beliefs are not shared by everyone and she is cruelly ridiculed. Her conclusions are extreme and don't allow for a lukewarm reaction. You can only either support her or reject her, a typical 8th house manifestation. Saturn is challenged by a square to Neptune in the 6th, the house of serving, and rules the ascendant. This is the confrontation between dissolution and ambiguity (Neptune) versus structure and boundaries (Saturn). Something solid (Saturn) tries to change its condition into something vaporous. Jupiter in the 12th, ruling the 9th and 10th, complements this square into a T-square. Since Saturn is the apex, the burden of responsibility always weighs heavier than the temptation of becoming all dreamy and befuddled. Jupiter wants to expand his horizons in the realm of the unconscious and hidden (12th house), fed by the urge to learn (9th house), following his calling (10th house). Saturn, as counteragent to both Jupiter and Neptune, always keeps on with the hard work, which accounts for Kübler-Ross' longevity. Saturn is a complex planet which can be experienced on three different levels. The lowest level is the one of passive inhibition, in which authority is projected on others. The second level is often one of over-compensation and unnecessary hardship, where performance pressure dominates the native's life. The third and most elaborate level brings one to accept one's limitations, while still wanting to accomplish one's goals.

This example of a T-square is indeed unusually challenging. Jupiter and Saturn play very different games and constantly rub against each other. Times of euphoria (Neptune) and optimism (Jupiter) are replaced by those of extreme hardship and pragmatism, bordering on pessimism (Saturn). Saturn simply has to take over the steering wheel and act as a responsible authority figure against Jupiter and Neptune. But how did Kübler-Ross manage to live under these extremely contradictory influences? A look at the trine between Sun/Pluto and Saturn gives the answer. A true powerhouse, always pushing through, even when the going gets tough. How very appropriate for someone who researches death.

Greta: I am the reincarnation of my dead sister

Shiatsu flashback

Berlin-Charlottenburg, summer of 2008. The local shops are doing a neighbourhood promotion with a tombola. Greta, a civil servant, aged 45, is intrigued. To win a prize, she firstly has to collect signatures in the shops and meet the owners. Being a typical Gemini, this is right up her alley. And hurray, she wins a shiatsu treatment. Greta is very partial to massages and relaxation exercises. After all, her job is all about brain work. The female shiatsu therapist seems very likeable and comes across as very competent. Under her experienced hands, Greta loosens up very quickly. But then, suddenly, something unexpected happens. A dramatic scene pops up before her inner eye; intense, vivid, powerful and eerie. A man carries the lifeless body of a little girl across a street. He looks totally desperate and forlorn, his mouth deformed to a pain distorted grimace. Greta can only see the man, not hear him, which makes everything even more dramatic. She immediately realises: "What I just saw was my father with my sister Maria, who was run over by a car before I was born".

A 'flashback' is a psychological phenomenon which involves an intense and unexpected memory of a specific situation, triggered by a key stimulus. Greta grew up with framed pictures of Maria all over the house, even though no one ever talked about her. Throughout her childhood, the sensitive girl could detect the underlying atmosphere of dejection and guilt.

What had happened? Her mother had left Maria, 4 years old, with her grandmother in the house, since it was a very hot day, and she had to work out in the fields. Maria's brother had gone to the village to play with

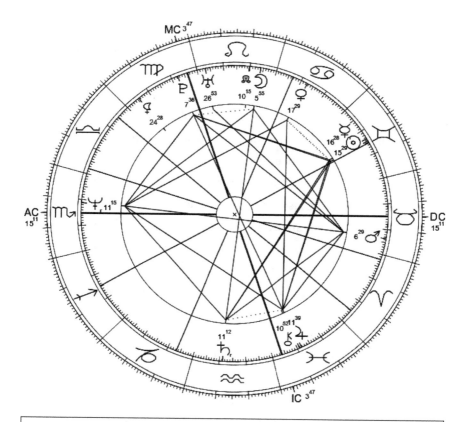

Greta, 6 June 1962, 17:45 UT, Soltau, Germany

8th house constellations

- Sun and Mercury retrograde in 8th as apex of T-square in mutable modality with Jupiter/Chiron in 4th and Pluto in 10th
- Mercury ruler of 8th and 10th
- Sun ruler of 9th (Leo intercepted)
- Pluto ruler of 1st
- Venus in 8th as ruler of 11th and 12th and part of a grand trine with Jupiter/Chiron and Neptune at ascendant

his friends. Suddenly the girl decided to go out and look for her brother. The grandmother looked away for only a very short moment, but it was too late. Maria had run in the street, which was normally very quiet, with hardly any traffic at all in the countryside. In this moment, a car drove by and hit her, killing her instantly. What followed was a long period of grief and shock. While the mother slipped into a depression, father and grandmother tried to pull themselves together and carry on. This had by no means been the only case of 'sudden death' in the family. Both grandfather and several uncles and cousins had committed suicide. When the mother got pregnant a few weeks after the incident, everyone could draw new hope. When the new baby, another girl, was born, the family felt she would heal the wound. Children are very sensitive, and Greta felt, right from the beginning, that it was her role to console the adults. A couple of years later, another sister followed. But Greta, oddly enough, always felt closer to the dead Maria, like there was some kind of an inexplicable connection.

After the shiatsu flashback incident, she reflects a lot on her family history and how it has always strongly, if subtly, influenced her own personality. Greta also feels that it is time to accept her own psychic powers, her ability to tune into 'other realities'. More and more, she loses her anxiety and ambivalence about this side of herself. A friend tries to hypnotise her, with success. During a session in which Greta regresses particularly far back in time, she sees Maria, who wants her to follow into a tunnel. "Do you see one or two lights?" the friend asks. "Only one," she replies. "There you go. This is the answer. Your dead sister and you, you are one and the same person." On the fiftieth anniversary of Maria's death, Greta is almost run over by a car, and not only once, but three times. From then on she is absolutely certain: "I am my sister." She feels her life has come full circle, or better, both her lives. The transformative shiatsu session has ignited a quest which will last for the rest of this incarnation. A quest to become whole again, and to own her shadow.

The chart: A high voltage circuit

Greta's chart displays a concentration of fixed modality. Particularly eye-catching is, among other aspect figures, an impressive Grand Cross. And the 8th house is one of the hot spots within this closely intertwined pattern. It contains, besides the Sun, also Mercury and Venus, who both rule two signs, thus making this house the destination for many other houses.

The Sun/Mercury conjunction forms the apex of a T-square with Jupiter and Chiron in the 4th house and Pluto in the 10th house. Jupiter/Chiron manifests itself in Greta's role as the family's comforter. This, however, comes at the cost of having to constantly confront one's own abysses (square Sun/Mercury in the 8th). Sun/Mercury also receives a testing quincunx angle from Neptune at the ascencdant, which makes her supersensitive and open to any kind of disharmonious vibrations. Since this is a quincunx, others might not be aware of these vibrations and rather pin it on the native's eccentricity. Scorpio rising is on his guard and likes to observe from a distance. Neptune, however, has a hard time with these Scorpio control issues and rather works with hypersensitive awareness. So there is a struggle between staying too reserved and being too open. Being able to absorb hidden feelings and needs does not necessarily imply that others welcome this empathic side of Greta. But can she really trust her perceptions? And how far does she want to go? A serious dilemma indeed.

2
A Place of Imbalance

Again, I tell you, it is easier for a camel to go through the eye of
a needle than for a rich man to enter the kingdom of God.
The Bible, Gospel of Matthew

These houses are so big and there is so much money involved. I
make myself feel better by thinking: They are not happy. You can't
have that much and be happy. They must be miserable.
Drag Queen Coco Peru, passing by luxury houses in Beverly
Hills - 'Coco goes to a Panettone fiesta' (YouTube)

Money and jealousy
In the German film *Die fetten Jahre sind vorbei* (2004) (The days of plenty
are numbered) a group of young urban guerrillas break into the houses of
the rich and wreak havoc. This vandalism expresses their deep frustration
about life's injustices. While some people live in decadent opulence, the
majority have to struggle. They feel that rich people need to be taught a
lesson, so they leave a note behind: 'You have too much money. Signed:
The legal guardians.'

Many believe that money is the key to happiness, or at least
to contentment. They dream about how fabulous it would be to live in
big houses, wear expensive clothes or go on luxury trips. Astrologically
speaking, this reflects on the relationship between the 2nd (own values and
talents) and the 8th house (values of others, shared values). If we see mostly
emptiness and want in our own 2nd, we might look hungrily at our 8th,
on the other side of the chart and try to get something from there. This

can become a fixed idea, also a domain of the 8th. Society can give us the feeling that we are worthless if we haven't got enough money, but also that we are not beautiful or talented enough. Wealth creates envy, which seems particularly relevant in Western culture. Since the dynamics of the 8th house are never simplistic, it holds true that wealth is also often despised. In Western culture we have a paradoxical relationship of love and hate with money.

In the 8th house all values, not just money, fall in and out of balance quite easily. This may concern legacies, taxes, debts and all sorts of dues. These dues are psychologically more complex than just material values. They are about energy in a more universal definition. We constantly give and receive energy, whether we are aware of this or not; intentionally or unintentionally. The laws of karma say that every deed, thought and feeling has an effect and can never get lost in the universe; the law of cause and effect. But every so often we might not feel that this law works to our advantage. We may feel that life treats us badly and unjustly and that in turn 'life owes us'.

The demon

'You cannot serve both God and mammon', it says in the New Testament. *Mammon* in Hebrew means 'money'. Money is associated with wealth, but also with greed, one of the seven deadly sins. The word *mamona* is Aramaic for 'wealth or possessions', derived from *aman*, which means 'what one relies upon.' To rely upon something is astrologically very much in line with the 2nd house. In Milton's *Paradise Lost* (1667) Mammon is one of the fallen angels, who together with Satan rebels against God. This is a vivid metaphor for how money can lead people astray and plunge them into deep crises, which brings us right into the 8th, the Plutonian house of self-conquest and transformation.

Apocalyptic times: Wall Street Crash 1929

All investors try to sell their shares at the same time, after their values plummet

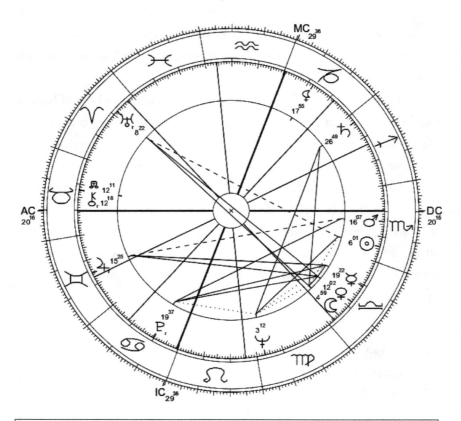

Black Tuesday, 29 October 1929, 17:32 EST, New York, RR:A

8th house constellations

- Saturn in Sagittarius in 8th house
- Saturn ruler of 9th and 10th
- Saturn has no major aspects, only a square with Moon (out of sign and a trine with Neptune (also out of sign)

Black Tuesday

New York City, 29 October 1929. The event chart shows Saturn in the 8th in Sagittarius as ruler of the 9th and 10th houses. This placement often signifies the settlement of a debt. The 'values of others' and/or 'shared values' (8th) may have become a burden and the delicate process of energy-exchange is out of balance. In this particular case, the imbalance has to do with beliefs and foreign affairs (9th), as well as with authority figures and power structures (10th). There will be restrictions (Moon square Saturn but out of sign) for the people (Moon) in their everyday life (6th). The Moon also receives an opposition from Uranus, so this incident is of a sudden, unexpected nature. The MC is at the critical degree of 29° Capricorn, so a complete shifting in goals will soon be happening when it moves to Aquarius. Jupiter, ruler of the 8th is placed in the 2nd house. This planetary connection could theoretically signify an exchange of values between 'the values of others or common property' (8th) in favour of 'own values' (2nd). But Jupiter is retrograde and in his sign of detriment, Gemini. This makes for a certain degree of confusion. Jupiter in the dual sign of communication has a capacity for going topsy-turvy. Being retrograde, it can signify losses and delays. To make matters worse, Jupiter receives a quincunx from highly charged Mars in Scorpio. The 150° angle often indicates that something is either happening too soon or too late. Mercury in Libra in the 6th and ruler of the 2nd is the apex of a T-square with Pluto and Lilith. The bottom line is 'looking for balance and compensation' (Libra) in order to manage everyday life (6th)', but the square with Pluto also signals a strong element of helplessness.

The bubble bursts

Due to a preceding speculative bubble, the Dow Jones index value for developments in the American stock market has reached dizzying heights. This leads to a wave of euphoria and a promise of everlasting prosperity. In this overheated climate many investors take out massive loans so that they can buy shares, hoping to resell them again with considerable profits. But as the roaring 1920s draw to an end, share values begin to fall again drastically, which makes investors realise how reckless everyone has been. As the capital flow begins to stagnate, a feeling of panic starts to spread. A crackling tension hangs in the air.

Only five days before the notorious 29th of October, brokers' nerves are shredded. Then the information seeps through that a well-known speculator in London has declared bankruptcy, which in turn leads to the withdrawal of British money from Wall Street. A domino effect kicks off and everyone wants to get rid of their shares. Values plummet dramatically and eventually the market breaks down. Loans can't be covered any more, so banks reclaim their money, which consequently causes investors to sell their security shares. Some values fall by 99% and some desperate investors even jump out of their office windows. Many fortunes completely disappear, companies close, and employees are sacked. The crisis gains momentum over the following years and reaches rock bottom in 1932 in the form of the Great Depression.

Client Karin: The sleeping house

Shared values

Karin contacts me in the summer of 2015. She is stuck in an unhappy marriage and has recently lost her job. She exudes an air of fatigue, a typical 8th house symptom. Until now everything has always come easily to her; husband, kids, home, job - the lot. The linchpin of Karin's troubles is her grandmother's house, which she had inherited. She and her husband Peter, a police officer, had had to raise a lot of money to renovate it and although they now co-own it, and the house is in a good condition, it never feels like a cosy home. After completing the major modernisations, they have now run out of money and don't do anything to decorate it, because Peter decrees that "there isn't any money left for this kind of unnecessary extravagance".

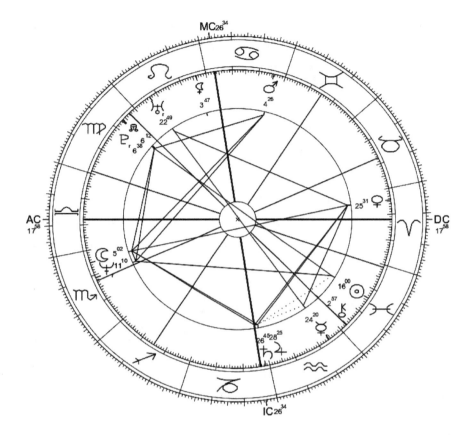

Karin, 6 March 1961, 20:45 UT Stockholm, Sweden

8th house constellations

- Venus, ruler of 8th, in Aries in 7th square Jupiter/Saturn in Capricorn at IC
- Venus trine Uranus in Leo in 10th
- Venus sextile Mercury in Aquarius in 4th
- Mercury opposition Uranus

After ten years it still looks as if they have just moved in, with naked light bulbs hanging from the ceilings and bare walls. The sterile and cold atmosphere reflects the stagnated state of their marriage. Karin is worn out, wants a separation and Peter out so that she can finally enjoy her house. But not only does he refuse to move out, he takes out his frustrations on her, because he claims he still loves her. But, alas, she doesn't love him. In fact she is having an affair with another man, which Peter chooses to ignore.

Jupiter and Saturn in the same boat
In Karin's chart both Jupiter and Saturn in Capricorn sit on the IC, which is a tricky, ambivalent placement. Saturn is in his domicile and Jupiter in his fall, but in the 4th the latter feels more at ease. They form a square with Venus in the 7th, ruler of the 1st and 8th, so this not only concerns home, roots and family (4th), but also Karin herself (1st), her marriage (7th) and shared values (8th). Jupiter and Saturn both want a say in these matters. And while Karin is blessed with her inheritance (Jupiter), she mostly feels the burden of the situation (Saturn). With the Sun in Pisces and Libra rising, she has a tendency to passiveness and finds it hard to face problems directly. Her Moon in Scorpio, on the other hand, has a capacity for revenge and stubbornness; 'the last man standing on the battle-field.'

Wanted: A beautiful home
Her childhood had been rather frugal in a very small and spartan flat, with her widowed mother and two brothers squeezed together. And yet Karin had always dreamed of having a beautiful and cosy home, filled with lots of friends. She inherits the house at the time of her first Saturn return, so it is apt that there is so much work involved. She tells herself, "The rest will follow later", and concentrates on her two kids. Then Peter begins to change. The formerly dynamic and charismatic man becomes moody, grumpy, demanding and aloof. This puts a strain on their relationship, and as the marriage deteriorates, so does the house. The garden is left unkempt

and wild, and junk accumulates in the cellar. The old furniture becomes even more faded and ugly and the whole atmosphere feels gloomy.

A compost heap

This is a typical 8th house story. Here we find all the processes of rotting, fading and deterioration. In the 8th something always has to die before it can transform and be reborn as something new. It works like a compost heap, in which micro-organisms disintegrate every single particle. Houses as symbols of shared values can also rot. Relationships can rot. Both need tending. Pandora's Box, another 8th house symbol, contains death, disease and all sorts of unexpected troubles, but also, deep down at its bottom, hope for mankind. Rotten material can transform over time into precious fertilizer. Relationships can transform and blossom, but both partners have to work on it. If one of them boycotts the process, the relationship can't improve. The same rule applies to houses. A house doesn't automatically feel like a home. Its occupants must put effort into making it comfortable and cosy. If one of the residents boycotts this process, the house will not feel welcoming.

Acting out

Peter stands in the way of her dream of the perfect home. Without a job, she now spends a lot more time at home. She likes to dream away on the sofa about what to do with the house, typical for a Pisces Sun. But as soon as Peter comes home, she panics. Will he be in a good mood? Will he punish her with silence? Or bully her? Get into one of his temper tantrums? He blames her for ruining his life and acts up. She, on the other hand, feels sorry for him, because he still loves her. And unlike her, he hasn't found a new partner. One of his 'specialities' is his 'educational treatment'. Whenever she has cooked something for herself, he puts the dirty pan in front of her on the coffee table. Or he throws her wet towel out of the bathroom window into the garden. A dilemma: What should she do?

Who takes the first step?

In the case of a legal separation from her husband, Karin would have to pay him for his share of the house, which she cannot afford. On the other hand, she doesn't want to move out either, because "...to move out everything in the house must be in order, which it isn't at the moment. My husband would throw everything in the dumpster, out of sheer spite. I cannot allow that and therefore I must stay and watch the house." This is clearly Saturn's voice. But Jupiter has also something to contribute to the conflict. Her eyes begin to sparkle when she speaks about the plans she has for the house, if she had it her own way. She would rent out the 1st and 2nd floors, live on the ground floor herself and create a happy community. She said, "I would love to fill my house with life and laughter, with all sorts of people, and I would never be alone".

A frustrated Venus

Venus is particularly troubled in this chart. Not only is it placed in Aries in the 8th (both in detriment), it also has to comply with the contradictory demands of Jupiter and Saturn in square in the 4th. This dynamic might account for her conciliatory attitude. "I don't think that my life is all that bad. After all, I am healthy, have a house and super kids." And if we look closer at the relationship between the three planets, it seems that Saturn in Capricorn keeps the upper hand, his message is: "Stop moaning, only the strong survive, just pull yourself together".

And there is another crucial square between Venus and the MC, which signifies problems between the areas of marriage (7th) and goals (10th). This is a typical angular house friction.

Venus is placed in the 7th as ruler of the 8th. This combination signifies a propensity for very intense partnerships. The partners tend to project their individual suppressed feelings, shadows and neuroses onto the other. It requires an enormous degree of self-control to show the partner your fears and weaknesses, because there is a lot of anxiety.

But Venus also receives two supportive angles. There is a sextile with retrograde Mercury in Aquarius in the 4th and a trine with Uranus in the 10th. Mercury and Uranus are in opposition. Together with Venus this aspect pattern is sometimes called an 'Ambivalence Figure', which enables her to see her problems from a certain neutral distance. If this is for better or worse remains to be seen...

Doris Day: A bitter legacy

The fatal year

Los Angeles, 20th April 1968. Doris von Kappelhoff, aka Doris Day, receives the shocking news that Martin Melcher, her husband and manager for over 15 years, has died in hospital from the implications of an enlarged heart. With the loss of her companion, Doris' whole world crumbles to pieces and plunges her into an abyss of desperation. Saturn transits her 8th house, where it will stay for 2 years; a cathartic journey. Pandora's Box opens up, and reveals other bad news. Martin had invested all her earnings of twenty successful years in show business in risky loans and toxic investments, leaving her bankrupt, and over half a million dollars in debt. She doesn't even own her house anymore. And it gets worse. As her manager he had full autonomy to sign her on to any project he considered lucrative. Now, to her dismay, she finds herself obliged to start immediately with filming a TV-series, *The Doris Day Show*, the existence of which she previously had no idea. Also, Melcher had already spent most of the upfront payment of the salary, so that she basically will have to work for free. There is no other option than to pull herself together and start to work. Doris, who is normally always cheerful and a hard worker, is almost numb with grief and disappointment. During filming she often bursts into tears on the set and has to seek refuge in her trailer.

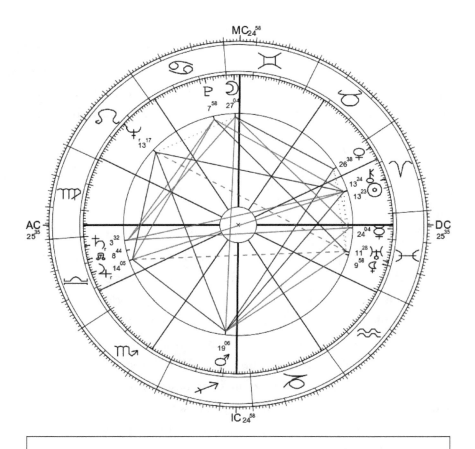

Doris Day, 3 April 1922, 16:30 CST, Cincinnati, Ohio, RR:AA

8th house constellations

- Venus in Aries in 8th, as ruler of 9th (Taurus) and 2nd (Libra)
- Venus quincunx ascendant
- Venus part of a grand trine with Mars and Neptune
- Venus sextile Moon and MC
- Mars ruler of 8th in Sagittarius in 3rd
- Mars square Uranus/Lilith
- Mars square ascendant
- Mars opposition Moon

The American dream

Doris Day's public image is very much in line with an Aries Sun and Virgo rising: hands on, energetic, daring, but modest and with a purpose. This combination is like the perfect formula to live the American dream: If you work hard enough (Virgo), and battle through (Aries), you will succeed whatever you do. The 1st house hosts both Jupiter and Saturn in Libra, albeit not in conjunction. Saturn is in exaltation, placed in the realm of fair play and diplomacy. In the 1st 'Father time' brings a capacity for discipline and self-sacrifice. And with Jupiter as housemate, these traits come across with a positive and effortless attitude. Her parents had been very opposite characters. The chart displays a close Sun/Chiron conjunction in the 7th in opposition to Jupiter and square to Pluto. Young Doris was devoted to her artistically talented but eccentric father (Sun/Jupiter), who indeed inflicted a wound (Chiron) in the 8-year-old girl when he left the family without saying goodbye. The Moon (mother) is in Gemini at the MC and receives an opposition from Mars in Sagittarius. Her mother Alma is a powerhouse, very pragmatic, reliable and supportive, also very goal-oriented.

Venus in muddy waters

Venus isn't exactly in her comfort zone in this chart. As to both sign and house, she is in detriment. On the one hand the planet of love has to dance to the rhythm of hasty and unwary Aries. On the other hand, in the Scorpionic 8th house, she is tainted with a smack of drama and passion. So for Doris, femininity always comes with a Martian twist. Venus rules the 9th (Taurus) and 2nd (Libra) houses. The ruler of the 9th in the 8th shows the influence of a mutual faith and vision (9th) for shared values (8th). Martin Melcher convinces Doris to become a Christian Scientist. She quits alcohol and cigarettes and willingly follows the 'mind over body' dogma of the sect. Ruler of the 2nd in the 8th, especially when Venus, planet of material goods, often comes with the attitude of 'What's mine (2nd) is ours (8th)'. The 2nd house rules our talents. Doris Day is the bread winner, while her husband takes up the role of manager (Mars in Sagittarius in the 3rd, the house of management). We also take into account that there is no earth in this chart besides the ascendant. So it comes as no surprise that Doris Day is in all things material a little bit naïve and careless.

Destructive partners

All her men are in show business and afraid of failure; replicas of her moody father. Her first husband, musician Al Jordan, who is also the father of son Terry, bullies her with his possessive jealously. Marriage number two is an almost exact repetition. There are even rumours of physical violence. She marries husband number three, Martin Melcher, in 1951, when she is already a big star. His Mars opposes her Mars, his Chiron sits on her Mercury and activates her powerful T-square. He takes her almost by storm. She really feels that with the tall handsome manager she has finally found her port in the storm. They establish a production company and he becomes her manager. Not only does she put her career in his hands, but also her family life. He sends Terry away to a boarding school, which Doris will never forgive herself for consenting to.

Her Sun in Aries in opposition to Jupiter is highly charged and tends to overdo things. Placed in the 7th together with Mercury, the chart ruler, this powerful placement is likely to be embodied by rather wilful partners. Already challenged by the conjunction with Chiron, the Sun also receives a square from Pluto in the 10th, which can signify control issues. The Sun is usually ashamed of Chiron, who in the myth has to hide inside a cave because he is so unsightly. The Sun might try to overcompensate for ugly duckling Chiron. It usually takes a long time to embrace his healing talents behind the rather unglamorous façade. The Sun is also part of a great trine in fire, also called 'Triangle of Grace', with Neptune and Mars. This brings on a passion for (artistic) self-expression and access to a deep source of optimism and resilience.

The dynamics of this pattern are: A wounded (Chiron) partner (Sun), highly ambitious (Jupiter) and battling for control (Pluto), while being driven by a constant source of energy (grand trine in fire).

There is a strong element of compulsive control and jealousy (Sun square Pluto) from the wounded partner (Sun/Chiron). Mars, as ruler of the 8th in the 3rd, means that being connected in daily life (3rd) is affected by the partnership and its shared values (8th). Mars is part of a T-square in mutable signs with Mercury in Pisces at the apex on the descendant and in opposition to Moon on the MC. This is a restless, nervous, flighty constellation. For ambitious and diligent Doris, life is a veritable hamster wheel. If she isn't on a film set, she is in a recording studio, never allowed to rest. Melcher makes her work like a horse. Or rather, she allows him to use her.

Christian Science does not believe in mourning. But this is exactly what she needs to do now. She renounces her faith. Venus in the 8th wants to face this loss with full force. Saturn conjuncts Venus and scrutinises the foundation (Saturn) of her marriage (Venus). And although she cannot bring herself to be really angry with Martin, she has to admit that she had idolized him. Instead she blames his financial adviser and takes the case to court. It will last for several years, but in the end, she is granted compensation.

In this crisis her mother Alma and her son Terry are pillars of strength. The three of them share a house. Then fate strikes again. In a motorcycle accident Terry almost loses his legs and has to convalesce for nearly a year. This is Doris' opportunity for atonement by nursing him back to health. Also, *The Doris Day Show* becomes a great hit and opens the door for a new career. Saturn leaves her 8th house. The deepest crisis of her life has turned out to be her biggest opportunity for self-growth.

Gustave Caillebotte

A life fully lived

Petit-Gennevillers, 21 February, 1894. Gustave Caillebotte, wealthy painter, photographer, patron and art collector, suddenly collapses and dies from pulmonary congestion in his garden. He is only 45 years old. Somehow he always had a premonition that death would come early. Maybe because of this, he had lived his life to the fullest, like a candle burning at both ends. He is a member of the so-called Impressionist art movement, albeit one who chose a more personal style. Unlike many of his fellow artists, he is of independent means and doesn't depend on what he earns from selling his paintings. Instead, he loves to buy dozens and dozens of canvases from his fellow artists whose work he so admires. Over a period of 20 years, he acquires a remarkable collection. Gustave Caillebotte is a somewhat mysterious figure in the history of art. His character is contradictory. While he is vigorously ambitious, self-confident and full of life, he is also modest and prone to melancholy at the same time. A typical 8th house personality, where intense pleasure and pain are inseparably interwoven in a person. The 8th house is the house of the values of others and of legacies. With a Sun in generous Leo his munificence makes the life of many struggling artists easier. Also, bringing his collection posthumously to a larger public will serve as the initial spark for creating momentum for many Impressionists. His own artistic contribution is re-evaluated much later, since the 1950s, after his descendants began to sell the family collection. His unique use of varying perspective is certainly magnificent and sets him apart from his fellow Impressionist artists. This specific use of perspective reminds me of the astrological quincunx angle of 150° degrees, which is so crucial for understanding the odd workings of the 8th house. Also typical for a plutonic influence is the subtle melancholic mood in his paintings, where something always lurks deep below the pretty surface.

The whiff of Death

There is something morbid and sad about the whole Caillebotte family; a curse, a subtle underlying whiff of death hanging over them. Gustave Caillebotte's father, the entrepreneur and self-made millionaire Martial Caillebotte (1799 – 1874), had been widowed twice and only one son had survived from these previous marriages. Consequently, he brings a heavy burden of grief and melancholy into his third and final marriage. And while he is a clever businessman and makes a fortune, he isn't quite able to enjoy his wealth. Life seems too fragile and unpredictable. It almost feels like death is constantly looking over his shoulder, ready to strike again at any moment. One can draw hypothesis about the father by the placement of the Sun in the chart. In his son Gustave's chart, the Sun is in the 8th house. This may signify that there is something tragic and aloof about the father figure which must also influence the native's own personality. Certainly, the very sensitive Gustave with the Sun in a trine and Moon in conjunction with Pluto must have felt his father's deep sadness. As an adult he displays a remarkable humility for life. And he has good reason to, for death visits the Caillebotte family again and again. Under the influence of his Saturn return, it dawns on young Gustave that he also won't grow old. It takes firstly his father, then his younger brother and then his mother, all within a period of only two years. But, instead of giving in to his sometimes severe periods of depression, he plunges himself into work.

The forgotten Impressionist

If asked to name famous impressionist painters, one would most likely come up with Renoir, Degas, Monet or Manet. Shimmering light, exciting use of colours, everything in motion, to catch each fleeting moment. Carefree protagonists who enjoy life or private intimate moments which invite us to take in a quickly passing moment. Lush nature, beautiful women, a vividly sensuous world. The painted moment is precious and ought to be cherished. This a world of the 2nd house, of Taurus and Venus. Many of those painting have found their way into our collective subconsciousness, reproduced in post cards and posters by the millions.

Caillebotte is the wealthy heir of a fabulous family fortune, so he doesn't have to starve like so many other artist friends. As a member of the noble and rich middle class, the new aristocracy of the French Republic, his life is set against the glamorous world of the French Belle Epoque. But he finds this hedonistic world decadent and shallow, and the prudish double standards of sexual morals appalling. Life in this rich elitist circle feels claustrophobic and fake, so he tries to find an escape in keeping busy instead of being idle. He also loves the solitude of nature and keeps to himself. In his chart the 8th house is packed with Sun, Venus, Mercury and Jupiter. If we think back about the Hellenistic take on the 8th house and the crooked unpleasant quincunx angle, we have an excellent blueprint of the life and art of Gustave Caillebotte. His *oeuvre* allows a captivating glimpse into his psyche. His paintings are in a more realistic style compared with most of his fellow Impressionists and have a unique flavour of melancholy and loneliness about them, without the typical Impressionist playful and light mood of joyful self-abandonment. His view on life in bourgois and industrialist Paris and his contemporaries is 'crooked' and critical, just as his Sun-Saturn-quincunx reflects. You never quite fit in, something always feels off and odd, you long to be in two places at the same time, you feel that time is working against you. He often uses this sort of 150° angle, reminiscent of the quincunx angle, from above or below which creates an interesting, unusual appeal. The scenes are unobtrusive, random, and yet have something private about them, the viewer doesn't quite know whether having a look is intrusive or welcome. His protagonists seem lonely, they don't interact with each other, and they appear preoccupied. The slightly uncomfortable quincunx angle adds to the ambivalence one has as a viewer, a very strange feeling.

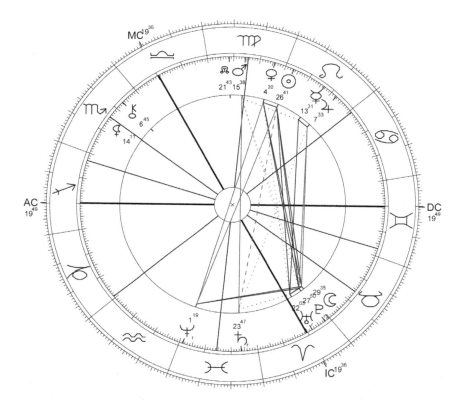

Gustave Caillebotte, 19 August 1848, 15:20 LMT, Paris, France

8th house constellations

- Sun, Mercury, Venus and Jupiter in 8th
- Moon, ruler of 8th, in 4th house conjunct Uranus and Pluto
- Sun trine Moon, Uranus and Pluto
- Sun co-ruler of 8th
- Sun quincunx Saturn in 3rd
- Venus opposition Neptune in 2nd

If you want to look up some of his paintings:

- *Les raboteurs de parquet* (1875)
- *Young man at his window* (1875)
- *Paris Street, Rainy Day* (1877)
- *Le Pont de l'Europe* (1876)
- *Le déjeuner* (1876)
- *Intérieur* (1880)
- *Un balcon* (1880)
- *Homme au bain* (1884)

Light and shadow of wealth

Gustave Caillebotte comes into money without having to work for it. And while this may sound very attractive in theory, it can indeed feel quite daunting. The Sun/Saturn quincunx suggests that the father relationship comes with a subtle strain. He is very rich when he comes into his inheritance but becomes richer still after the death of his brother and mother. He only has to share the family fortune with his beloved brother Martial. They are now both millionaires, and could live a life of idleness and decadence, but they both feel that with freedom also comes responsibility (Sun/Saturn). Gustave feels ambivalent, the flip side of what the 8th house has in store. Is there a certain degree of shame at work? Do the brothers maybe have a guilty conscience? Most of the artists Gustave meets are living in very reduced circumstances, barely able to make ends meet. Since the huge inheritance comes with a bitter taste on account of having to part with beloved family members, it is hard to feel carefree about money. He would prefer not to have the money and instead still have his family alive. Here we can trace the tight interaction between houses 4 and 8. Painting is only one of many pursuits in which he excels.

Typical for someone with a lot of fire in their chart, he tries to challenge himself mentally and physically. He is very athletic, a passionate rower who also dabbles successfully in building boats. Yes, he is a man of independent means. And no, he doesn't have to earn a living. But he keeps himself very busy, all the time. This might be the Mars in Virgo at the MC in opposition with Saturn in Pisces. This placement of the red planet suggests a life of aiming for perfection at any cost ('Idle hands are the devil's workshop'). Saturn in Pisces on the other hand has a hard time doing anything only remotely selfish and wants to serve other people who are less fortunate. In an opposition this has the makings of a restless and driven personality.

His Sun in Leo and Sagittarius rising might account for a certain zest for life, but Pluto and Saturn leave a stronger imprint. Not only does he finance art exhibitions, but he also even hammers the nails for the canvasses into the walls personally. Saturn rules his 2nd house, the house of talents. But in altruistic Pisces these talents are for the benefit of others. Pisces is also a very artistic sign. Saturn in the 3rd stands for taking networking, PR and management very seriously.

His secret private life

Although Gustave Caillebotte never marries, he doesn't live alone. Apparently, it is important for him to have company at home. The Moon rules his 8th house and is placed at the critical degree of 29°Aries, in the 4th house, in conjunction with Uranus and Pluto. While Pluto craves intimacy and transformation, Uranus wants freedom and makes itself known by sudden disruptions. The Moon in the 4th wants to take root, even in the impatient and restless sign of Aries. So, there is good reason to suspect at least some degree of ambivalence with everything regarding the 4th house, including family, home and privacy. The 4th house also represents psychic processes. Ruler of the 8th in the 4th can be decoded as: Legacies (8th) influence family life as well as inner psychic self-consciousness (4th). Feelings which arise by this interaction are ambivalent (Uranus/Pluto) and prone to mood swings (Moon in the 4th).

He lives with his mother until her death, then with his brother Martial until Martial gets married. In his last years he lives with Charlotte Berthier, a woman from the lower class, to whom he leaves a sizeable annuity. His best and closest friend is his brother Martial. But Martial's wife refuses to receive Gustave in her home, so there must have been something scandalous and improper about his lifestyle. What's more, there are certain homoerotic undertones in some of his pictures. But we know nothing concrete about his sexuality at all, also typical for the 8th house. Also, his relationships with his artist friends deteriorate over the time. They are a difficult bunch and fall out time and time again. For a person with Sun in the 8th and Moon in the 4th superficial relationships are unsatisfactory, so he rather chooses to stick with a few very reliable friends.

A critical observer

With the Sun in Leo trine Pluto/Moon in Aries and Sagittarius rising, it is no surprise that Gustave is physically strong and virile. In photographs he looks charismatic and provocative, standing with legs apart, his posture tense, ready to jump any minute. But this demonstrative strength is only a façade. He suffers from mood swings, which will increase towards the end of his life. Melancholy will finally get the upper hand and push him into solitude, which will eventually turn into loneliness. During his final years he will become a recluse.

His art mirrors the state of his psyche. His paintings have nothing of the lightness and effervescence of the other Impressionists, whose protagonists, nature and urban background evoke a feeling of joy. His style is much more realistic and serious, somewhat mysterious and melancholic. His protagonists often find themselves out of the way, not part of the crowd, rather watching than participating, being wrapped up inside of their own inner world. They are busy rowing, knitting, sanding parquet, reading a newspaper. They avoid eye contact with the painter and consequently with the viewer. To keep the viewer from becoming too close and intrusive, he must look at the picture from an uncomfortable 150° quincunx angle, from above over the protagonist's shoulder or from the ceiling. The effect is remarkable, one feels peace and quiet and tension at the same time.

The legacy: unhealthy art

Following Caillebotte's death, his estate, in keeping with his will, is a generous donation to the French State, which is a big surprise for everyone. The artist had drafted his will early in his life, aged 29, during his first Saturn return, after the untimely passing of his brother, Rene. His will reads, "I give to the French State the paintings which I have; nevertheless, since I want that this donation be accepted and in such a manner that the paintings go neither in an attic nor in a provincial museum, but... in the Luxembourg Museum and later in the Louvre Museum, it is necessary that a certain time passes before execution of this clause..."

The donation fuels controversy, which brings to light how resistant to avant garde art and artists the French Academy still is, even in 1894. Academy officials attempt to prevent the transfer of the works by Impressionists to the French National Museum. The works had been consistently refused admission to the official Salons through the years and the art establishment strongly opposed acceptance of what they refer to as "unhealthy" art. These works contain what is now considered some of the most important examples of modernist art of the late-19th century in France.

3
Sex and Seduction

I coveted you. I had no right to want you - but I reached out and took you anyway. And now look what's become of you! Trying to seduce a vampire.
Stephanie Meyer, 'Eclipse'

Oh yes, certainly her daughter must be seduced. But that will not be enough: she must be ruined too.
Pierre Choderlos de Laclos, 'Les Liaisons dangereuses'

The groin areas come under the rulership of the eighth house including the genitalia and organs of reproduction, indicating perhaps that within the seed of death there is a promise of new life.
Wanda Sellar, 'The Consultation Chart'

The two sides of sex

If we look for sex in a chart, we have to explore the 5th and the 8th houses. Revealingly, they form a natural square to each other, both being fixed. This, for starters, tells us a lot about the astrological interpretation of sex. The 5th house is a fire house, forming a playful, optimistic, romantic background for flirting, self-expression and finding pleasure in the company of others. Any planets in the 5th, provided they don't only receive challenging aspects, can be a source of narcissistic feed. Sexuality in the 5th means being in love with love, testing our own attractiveness. It is not necessarily about the act itself, but more a kind of foreplay or first flush of romance. The 5th house is where children are placed, our own biological children as well as brain children, creativity and our own childish, innocent, regressive playfulness.

The 8th house bears a very different taste of sex. It is a fixed, water house and thus deeply involved with emotions. Yes, it is also about seduction and flirtation, but in a much less harmless way. Water needs actual soul contact, wants to merge and experience intimacy. In the house of Pandora's Box, we get so close to each other that the boundaries of our egos dissolve. In *Beyond the Pleasure Principle* (1920), Sigmund Freud concludes that all instincts fall into two major categories: life (Eros) or death (Thanatos) instincts. And guess what? In the 8th these instincts can become intertwined and messed up. In mythology, Eros and Thanatos are brothers, reminding us how close together pleasure and pain can be. The French call an orgasm *La petite morte*, the little death. We all look in others for something to make us whole, fill our void, give our existence a meaning. All our lust and yearning are projected on potential partners in sex, love or intimate friendship. This dynamic inevitably has to lead to some sort of disillusionment and disappointment. In times of quick and easy dating and sex apps, it seems like we can pick and choose a partner like a piece of furniture or a pizza topping, exactly according to our taste. The reality, naturally, looks completely different. Dealing with the knowledge that others are not how we wish them to be is uphill work, and requires a lot of mature adaptation of reality. This is basically what the 8th house is all about; constantly facing the truth behind the illusion and projection.

Loss of control

Close, intimate relationships can involve heavy and painful battles of will. Ego clashes with ego. Hiding behind facades no longer works, the mirror of projection cracks from side to side. And yet these fights, if properly resolved, can bring a much more satisfactory quality into a relationship. It can be reassuring to know each others' defects - in good times and in bad; all the little touchy points. One does not only love the other person's sunny sides. The 5th house, if you will, is the courtship, the flirting, the foreplay. The 8th house is the actual act, the actual getting to know each other, the clash of values and feelings. Taboos need to be broken and boundaries crossed. This can bring about transformation. The 8th house encompasses hidden agendas and dangerous, self-destructive, often unconscious triggers. An 8th house symbol is a pond with murky, brackish water, where one cannot see the bottom. The surface is still and motionless, while underneath there are all sorts of plants and fish. You need to stir the pot, so to speak, to bring everything out in the open. Stirred-up feelings are often necessarily mixed up and chaotic. Feelings of love, tenderness and protectiveness mingle with hate, envy, spite or desperation. This is normal and even healthy. We are all mixed up to some extent, and when two people get together it can get seriously messy and intense! The urge to control one's own feelings and those of others might be natural, to some extent, but also highly unrealistic, so why bother at all?

A relationship, therefore, is about giving and receiving, often with an uneven balance. Ideally, both partners give and receive. The 8th house can also have a mental quality to it, as it hosts images and fixations. By thinking of someone else, sending this person energy, or hoping to receive energy from them, we can become stuck, or even obsessed. This can apply to people who we know personally or even total strangers. Or even dead people. Thoughts and feelings can remain as memories for a very long time, one can even live off them.

Sex and addiction

Sexual addiction, contrary to what many might think, has very little to do with pleasure or sexual satisfaction. For the addict, also known as a sexaholic, the addiction rather brings a loss of self-esteem; it destroys relationships and threatens work life and mental health. The afflicted often suffers from a deep inner feeling of emptiness and futility. Sex is a means to numb a feeling of desperation, often accompanied by alcohol, drug and substance abuse.

Actor Charlie Sheen (*Hot Shots*, *Two and a Half Men*), with Moon in the 8th opposite Jupiter, enjoyed success right from a very young age. He lived his life to extremes and always wanted more (Jupiter) of everything. Once the highest-paid actor on the planet, he finally fell from grace in a drug-fuelled, alcohol-soaked spiral of self-destruction. In his time of greatest need, his family stuck with him and supported him. He finally got his life back together, with the aid of therapy and rehabilitation.

History is full of examples of powerful men under the spell of women (and men) who sexually manipulated them. The French King Louis XV (Jupiter in the 8th, square the Sun in the 12th), debilitated great-grandson of magnificent Louis XIV, let his mistress, Madame de Pompadour (Uranus in the 8th), deal with the politics while he lived a life of idle leisure.

Client Hannah: Incest

A dissolute evening with consequences...

It has got late. All the others are already in bed. Hannah and her brother Richard are the only ones left. So far, the family outing with an overnight stay has been surprisingly harmonious, what a relief. 22-year-old Hannah feels rather tipsy and in a euphoric mood. Richard, her senior by only one year, is also relaxed and looks quite happy. Richard has always been her most important contact within the family, much more important than their parents. Alcohol has been flowing rather freely over the evening, not at all unusual in this family. But this evening feels somehow different for the young woman. All of a sudden, she feels overwhelmed by a strange and never-before-experienced kind of desire and lust. She wants to be near to her brother; nearer than normal, nearer than ever before. She wants to own him, possess him, take him in, ever so deeply. And then it happens. She seduces him and he allows it. It is every bit as satisfactory as she had hoped, also for him. Afterwards, they never talk about it again. Not ever. It becomes their little secret. In retrospect, the mature woman, by now in her late 60s, completely sympathises with her actions as a young woman.

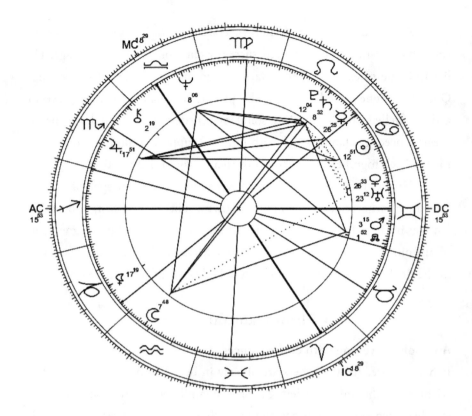

Hannah, 5 July 1947, 19:35:00 UT, Liebenburg, Germany

8th house constellations

- Mercury retrograde in 8th as ruler of 6th, 7th and 9th
- Moon as ruler of 8th in 2nd, Sun as ruler of 8th (Leo intercepted) in 7th
- Moon part of a grand trine in air with Mars and Neptune
- Saturn/Pluto in 8th opposition 8th house ruler Moon
- Chiron as apex of a T-square with Saturn/Pluto and Moon

"I really wanted to possess him, to dominate him, to merge with him and never let him go."

Violence and addiction as a family issue

Alcohol always plays a fatal role in her family. Everyone drinks, almost all the time. Booze is, astonishingly, given the hard, post-war times, with food rationing and shortages everywhere, always available; mostly home-made schnapps.

Hannah grows up in an old farmhouse. After the war, housing is scarce, and people often find themselves crammed together in confined spaces. Hannah's family, like many others, are also obliged to take in paying tenants. Country life, at least on the surface, seems idyllic and peaceful, much less bleak than in the bombed cities. Under the surface, however, there is an abyss of pain and despair, constantly threatening to erupt into violence. Her father, grandfather, uncle and every other male in the village have come back from the war deeply traumatised. Back at home, where times had been horrible as well, nobody wants to hear their sad war stories. So the lid has to be kept firmly on all their frustrations.

Her mother suffers from depression and has taken to the bottle. This means trouble for the children, for alcohol has an unpredictable effect on her. Sometimes she would be in a good mood, at other times she would become aggressive and violent. In the latter case, she would always take it out on the children. Her prime target is Richard, the eldest. During these beatings the boy always stays calm and stoic. His pride forbids him to show any sign of weakness in front of his odious mother. Hannah is always summoned to witness and watch every stroke. She cries and screams desperately, so loudly that the neighbours have to come and intervene. There are other punishments, too. The freezingly cold and dark cellar, a typical 8th house symbol, is really scary with its musty smells and strange noises. Time and again the unpredictably moody mother locks the children away, for no apparent reason.

Traumatic experience

At the age of five, Hannah gets to witness a terrible accident. The family is assembled around the table to have supper. At Hannah's side sits her two-year-old little sister in her nightgown, which is much too big for her. They are having tea. The water is heated up in an immersion coil. The electric cable hangs loosely over the sofa, the pot with the hot tea is on the table. And suddenly it happens. The fidgety little girl gets caught up in the cable with her nightgown. The pot topples over and pours its boiling hot content over her back. The ambulance is called, but arrives too late; she is beyond help and dies during the night from her fatal burns.

After this traumatic experience, the relationship between the parents deteriorates to the point where they totally ignore each other. The father falls into a deep depression and loses every interest in conjugal intercourse. The mother, on the other hand, is sexually less indifferent and now obliged to look elsewhere for potential sexual partners. The neighbourhood bakery employs apprentices who lodge with Hannah's family and are an easy target. Hannah often finds bank notes on her mother's bed, obviously the remuneration for the young men. Later she learns that also her grandmother had resorted to this arrangement when she was younger.

Since the affectionate and emotionally needy girl feels so rejected by her parents, she also has to look elsewhere for affection. The problem is that affection is always linked with the exchange of favours and never comes unselfishly. It is the little things in life which bring joy to Hannah; to sit on a lap or to get tucked into bed, to receive precious gifts such as Micky Mouse comics or chewing gum. But every situation can suddenly become dangerous. Time and again, Hannah has to defend herself against all sorts of assaults; from her grandfather, her uncle, the tenants, the neighbours. She is clever and always manages to get out of these dangerous situations by screaming, scratching, biting or threatening to tell. "It's a wonder that I never got raped," she reminisces.

Inside the darkroom

She follows an apprenticeship with her uncle, who runs a pharmacy. It involves all sorts of activities, such as developing pictures in a darkroom. A darkroom is a powerful image of the 8th house, not only on account of the obvious darkness, but also because of the transformative process. The uncle is rather exuberant with his impressive height and obese figure. He is constantly sweating and has bad breath. She has to assist him in the darkroom, which, involuntarily, necessitates close body contact - a scary and highly uncomfortable situation. Apart from feeling disgusted, she fears that at any moment he could suddenly assault her. But she makes it clear that she wouldn't allow this without putting up a fight. The uncle, who can't cope with the rejection, resorts to plan B. One evening after he closes the shop, he blocks the door so that she can't get out and forces a conversation on her. He tells her repulsively vivid details of all sorts of venereal diseases. She is horrified and eventually shakes him off, which is not easy. For the rest of her life, these images will stick in her brain.

In contrast, her prudish aunt forbids Hannah to open the drawer with the label 'rubber articles'. When a customer asks for a pack of rubbers, to his bemusement she offers him a pack of single-use rubber rings. Later, of course, she gets acquainted with the true meaning of rubbers. She also learns of the existence of bordellos and that many honourable, seemingly unblemished men in the community regularly frequent these establishments. Everyone seems obsessed with sex, but nobody talks about it, it's taboo. Welcome to the 1950s...

Am I good or evil?

Hannah is a creative young woman who dreams about fulfilment in a career, but she also longs to be wife and mother. Her loveless childhood has left her desperate for affection and companionship. She meets her future husband when she is very young. She is absolutely certain she is in love with him, but then again, she might have made it all up. An illusion? Neither of them take marital fidelity too seriously and both have a variety of sexual partners. Alcohol also plays a crucial rule. When she is drunk, the floodgates open and she feels powerful and gorgeous, like she could have any man she wants. Normally shy and insecure, she now transforms into a vixen, aggressively flirting with and seducing as many men as possible, just for fun. There are no boundaries or moral rules. She sleeps with her girlfriends' husbands or total strangers, it doesn't matter, as long as it is unorthodox and wild. Her husband, by contrast, is not adventurous at all and is content with the traditional missionary position. She soon gets bored. The birth of her son re-energises the relationship for a time, but then, during her Saturn return, she divorces her husband.

Now she plunges into a deep depression and loses all her drive. She accuses herself of being a failure and feels utterly guilty and shameful. She also tells herself that she is a bad mother, selfish and unreliable. Again, she numbs herself with sex and alcohol. The fact that men seem to find her desirable gives her a delusory feeling of power. Alcohol is a very effective stimulant, making her feel elated and happy. The inevitable hangovers, however, hit her harder and harder, and each time she feels even lower than before. A vicious cycle, the only things that help are the next drink and the next man. Additionally, there are financial quarrels with the family; mostly inheritance matters, which last for decades - typical for the 8th house.

Hannah is a tough cookie and has survived all these hardships more or less graciously. Her job as a fashion designer and her usually positive attitude have helped her to struggle through. Her relationships with her family are far from harmonious, but they found a way of dealing with each other. She has also found her peace with her son, who denies that she was a bad mother. Her absolute joy is her grandson, whose Sun is on her Venus in Gemini.

But, typically for an 8th house problem, the destructive dynamics in her chart can rise up again when she least expects it. Money troubles, the temptations of alcohol, and a tendency for bitterness and vindictiveness can take over. Then, she takes a deep breath and tries to stay optimistic. Never an easy task...

Exit strategy: Neptune

The 8th house in her chart has two rulers. The main ruler is the Moon, the second ruler is the Sun, given Leo is intercepted. The Moon is in the 2nd house, the place of self-esteem and talents, opposite Saturn/Pluto in the 8th. This combination is a very challenging one. Moon in Aquarius can feel cut off from its emotions. Its placement in the 2nd often indicates fluctuations in self-esteem as well as in the native's finances. Saturn, on the other hand, feels ill at ease in Leo, the sign of its detriment, where the need for restriction and hard work rather clashes with the sign of splendour and self-importance. Saturn, in this fixed fire sign, can leave a big dent in the native's pride. The pairing with Pluto, planet of transformation, passion and power, creates in its opposition from the 8th a mixture of mistrust, jealousy, anxiety and the urge to control, which can even have neurotic tendencies.

Hannah's lesson from her childhood is that opening up emotionally to other people (Moon), can quickly become dangerous, since others might take advantage and use her for their own needs (Moon opposition Saturn/Pluto). The solution, or rather, exit strategy, must be of a Neptunian nature, since the planet of dreams and escapism forms a trine with the Moon and a sextile with Saturn/Pluto in the 8th. In the 8th, Saturn/Pluto create feelings of guilt where sex is involved, but might also create something strangely sexually loaded and impelling. The native might consequently be powerless against her urges, while simultaneously feeling dirty and ashamed. These strong contradictory feelings can best be dealt with by suppression (Moon in Aquarius).

The problem with suppressed emotions is that they don't go away. They live on in the unconscious and can pop up at any inappropriate moment. Neptune, the knight in shining armour who can make everything appear so effortless and pleasant, forms a grand trine with Mars in Gemini and the Moon. A grand trine in air can make one feel quite unattached from any emotional dramas in life. A cool and soothing breeze to bring distraction. But the cat bites its own tail. Neptune is in the 9th, and its house ruler, Mercury, is in the 8th. Mercury is retrograde in touchy and emotional Cancer and entangled in a nervous quincunx to the ascendant. So, the path to inner growth is: slow processing (Cancer) of old trauma (8th house) in therapy, with the goal to mentally grasp experiences (Mercury).

Chiron, who signifies wounds in the chart, holds a key position at the MC, as the apex of a T-square with Moon and Saturn/Pluto. To find one's vocation in life (MC) can only be achieved by confronting deeper wounds and giving comfort to others (Chiron). Pluto as ruler of the MC is in the 8th. By facing fearful odds (Chiron at the MC in Scorpio), Hannah had to adapt and reinvent herself time after time, while simultaneously staying true to herself.

The closet: An 8th house symbol

In many countries around the world, being gay is still a crime. So is it any wonder that so many men and women hide their sexuality and prefer to stay 'in the closet'? The closet is a vivid symbol for living a lie, which seems to fit best with the 12th house, rather than the 8th. After all, the 12th is the place in the chart where things are hidden and suppressed, mystified and unconscious. So far, so good. But if we shed some light on all the implications, which both staying in the closet and also coming out of it can have, we simply must make a beeline for the 8th house. It is the house of the values of others, crime, taboos, boundary crossing, sexuality and transformation. The values in the 8th influence our own values in the 2nd house. And consequently, whenever the values of society and family ban homosexuality as wrong, then this must necessarily influence the native's own values and self-esteem (2nd house).

Homosexuality has always been one of Hollywood's biggest taboos. Even today, the fact that an actor is openly gay can limit his career considerably. Ironically, gay characters have become increasingly popular, but that is where the good news ends, because they are overwhelmingly played by straight actors. The implication being that a gay actor playing a gay character wouldn't be a great achievement. Straight actors, on the other hand, are praised highly for their 'braveness' to tackle a role, which is so very much out of their comfort zone. Afterwards these actors often go on and on about how hard it was having to physically touch another man and pretend any sort of 'softer' feelings for them, in order to preserve their butch masculinity.

Openly gay actor Sir Ian McKellen (*Lord of the Rings*) is one of many who has been critical of Hollywood's attitude to gay actors in the past. He has pointed out that no openly gay man has ever won the Academy Award for Best Actor, while straight actors have taken home the prize for playing LGBT roles on more than one occasion. Tom Hanks won it for *Philadelphia* and Sean Penn scooped it for *Milk*. In total, 52 straight people have been Oscar-nominated for playing gay characters, including Cate Blanchett for her portrayal in *Carol*, in which she plays a middle-aged married woman in the 1950s who is attracted to a young girl.

Victim

The 1961 British *neo noir* suspense film *Victim* was ground-breaking, as for the first time it used the explicit term 'homosexual'. In fact, the whole film is about this subject. In it, Dirk Bogarde courageously plays a successful married lawyer who becomes personally involved in a blackmail case. Instead of playing along and paying for remaining unexposed, he kicks off an investigation. The film reflects on this widespread phenomenon of blackmail by showing the desperation of some of the film's characters. Bogarde seeks cooperation with the police so that the gangsters can be arrested and be put under lock and key. His personal sacrifices are considerable. He has to give up his career as a lawyer, and his wife divorces him.

Bogarde was himself a closet homosexual, which makes this film so very poignant. In the 1950s he had been the biggest British film star, and his career after *Victim* flattened noticeably. He took a huge risk with this role, but never regretted it. The early 1960s saw a growing interest in sexual liberation, which by 1965, under the Uranus/Pluto conjunction, had become a mass phenomenon.

His chart doesn't have planets in the 8th, but its ruler, Saturn (restrain), is retrograde in Virgo in the 5th house (acting) and has no aspects. His 1961 solar return displays a full 8th house, with a Moon/Uranus conjunction, with a sextile to his MC and trine to his ascendant, which indicates a need for emotional liberation and transformation. This is an interesting placement for someone who is so crucial in breaking this particular taboo. Both houses rule sexuality and seduction. In contrast, he never admitted his own homosexuality publicly, although it was an open secret.

Only very few openly homosexual actors have managed to keep a high profile in Hollywood. Some of the most well-known actors who never dared to come out are Montgomery Clift, Rock Hudson and Anthony Perkins. The 1950s all-American dream boy, actor and singer Tab Hunter, however, decided at age 74 to come out of the closet and publish his autobiography *Tab Hunter Confidential: The making of a movie star*.

Tab Hunter Confidential

"I was a pretty big movie star in the 1950s. Oh, and another thing: I was — am — gay. That wasn't the sort of topic that one spoke freely about back then, since it could spell the end of one's career..."

'Tab Hunter Confidential: The Making of a Movie Star' (2005)

Better get it from the horse's mouth

Los Angeles, 2005. Former actor Art Gelein, aged 74, aka Tab Hunter, the 'Sigh Guy' in the 1950s, has just published his memoirs. With this, he officially comes out of the closet. Hunter had always been a very private person who didn't want to discuss his sexuality, but now feels that it is high time to come out. There are rumours that someone intends to write a tell-it-all story about him, so he decides he'd rather tell the story himself. Better get it from the horse's mouth than from the horse's ass. *Tab Hunter Confidential – The Making of a Movie Star* becomes a bestseller, and ten years later is also made into an award-winning documentary.

Once he was one of the most famous Hollywood stars whose sexy, yet wholesome all-American looks made him box office gold. His career, however, went downhill when he decided to leave his studio, Warner Brothers, and seek artistic freedom under his Saturn return at the age of 28. He died in 2018, only days short of his 87th birthday, having been able to finally live his life as an openly gay man for over a decade. He is survived by his partner of 35 years, Allan Glaser. There had been other men at his side over the years: fellow actor Tony Perkins, dancer Rudolf Nureyev and figure ice skater Ronnie Robertson, to name but a few.

The uber-masculine star as product of the old Hollywood-system

Hunter is one of the last surviving stars of the 1950s Glamour era, when stars were the products of the studio contract system. They have to project

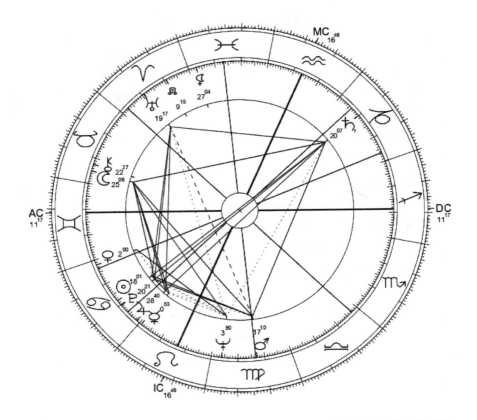

Tab Hunter, 11 July 1931, 03:00 EDT, New York, RR:DD

8th house constellations

- Saturn retrograde in Capricorn in 8th as ruler of 8th
- Saturn as base of a kite, with an opposition to Sun/Pluto in 2nd and a grand trine in earth with Moon/Chiron in 12th and Mars in 5th
- Saturn involved in a T-square with Sun/Pluto and apex Uranus in 11th

a certain persona, which often strongly contrasts with their real personality. Fan magazines sell stars as products and projection figures for the huge consumer target of post-war generation teenagers. The girls, especially, demand male stars that they can fantasise over. Usually this fantasy would end up in a proper marriage with the boy next door. A male star has to at least give the impression of being an eligible bachelor; alas a gay star, however handsome, could never be part of this deal. In his book, Hunter sheds light on his experiences within the studio system. It is a tale of selling your soul to the devil, modest and reflective, with a refreshing touch of self-irony.

As befits an 8th house biography, his life is a real rollercoaster. Constantly driven by anxiety, his strict upbringing teaches him to always pull himself together. Don't let anyone become too intimate and stay on your guard. But this attitude, astrologically largely fuelled by a kite figure with Saturn in Scorpio as a base in the 8th house also leads him, more than once, to the brink of total mental and physical exhaustion.

Super-charged power circuits

His chart displays tightly interwoven aspect patterns which combine both constructive, easy influences as well as very challenging and stressful ones. They set the scene for a personality which is both blessed with certain gifts, but also has to suffer under a lot of pressure. The price of livng inside the closet. No wonder, since Tab Hunter's Sun is very much involved. In a conjunction with Pluto, it is in the second house of talents and self-esteem, but opposite retrograde Saturn in Scorpio in the 8th. The Sun also sits at the head of a kite.

With Saturn in the 8th, control issues are enormously important in the native's life, like living in a pressure cooker with a lot of passion and repression stored up inside. One detects a certain tension in his appearance. His large, greyish green eyes are piercing and have a sense of suspicion about them. While coming across as very self-confident and down-to-earth, he is deeply shy under all the joviality. A very special brand of subtle vulnerability.

Living behind a wall of angst

The apple doesn't fall far from the tree. His mother is highly strung and unpredictable; always under a lot of pressure. Gertrude Gelien, born 5th January 1909, in Hamburg (birth time unknown), Germany, is very independent. When her husband becomes more and more abusive towards her, she leaves him for good, taking her two sons with her. Raising them by herself is hard, particularly during the Depression and war time, and she has to juggle two jobs just to make ends meet. Tab's feelings for his mother are complicated. Although he loves and worships her, he is also afraid of her temper tantrums. He can feel her inner pain and sorrow, but is unable to help her. His Moon/Chiron conjunction in the 12th is a vivid expression of a deep compassion (Chiron) with a helpless mother (Moon in 12th). Gertrude's chart displays a Sun/Uranus conjunction in opposition with Neptune and a trine with Jupiter. This constellation directly sits on Art's Sun/Pluto/Saturn opposition. At times she develops severe psychological problems and Tab has to commit her to a clinic where she is given electric shock treatment, which fills him with guilt. Eventually she recovers and the two share a close, if difficult bond for the rest of her long life.

He longs for a father-figure to look up to, other than his beloved older brother. But there must be something really dark about his father, because Gertude starts to shiver out of fear as soon as his name is mentioned. Tab travels to New York to meet him, but he cruelly refuses to see him, which hurts the boy deeply. This is a typical Sun/Pluto/Saturn situation. The Sun is a symbol for the father figure as well as the core identity. Pluto in conjunction with the Sun can make one feel the helpless underdog, craving in vain guidance and encouragement from an absent father. Instead Tab hero-worships his older brother Walt, who tries to encourage him to come out of his shell of extreme shyness. He feels out of place, which often comes with Uranus in the 11th. The odd one out. The black, or in this case, pink sheep which just doesn't fit it with the herd.

At school, the dashingly handsome Art, with his piercing big blue eyes and blond hair, is constantly chased by the girls. Even as a child he has a magnetic aura, which, in the form of Sun/Pluto in the sensuous physical 2nd house, gleams under the friendly boy-next-door Gemini ascendant. And while other (straight) boys might have enjoyed this hysterical adoration, young Art Gelein feels extremely uncomfortable. At times, there is no other escape from the hordes of female admirers than to lock himself inside an empty classroom. This is his first taste of how it feels to be the projection of female fantasies. He is full of anxiety and tension, an echo of his mother's controlling and highly-strung nature. She teaches him that whenever there is something bad you have to push it from your mind.

Pushed into the closet

He has his first homosexual experience as a teenager, which leaves him with the feeling of overwhelming guilt. Things go from bad to worse when he seeks guidance in confession. The result is disastrous, because the priest condemns the young gay man as a sinner, so he turns away from the church and his faith and decides to suppress his feelings and sexuality in future.

The man with the Midas touch

The movies are his little world of escapism, but he had never thought about becoming an actor himself until he is discovered by an agent. Art Gelien is introduced to Henry Willson, a gay Hollywood talent agent, who is part of the so-called beefcake craze of the late 1940s and 1950s. He is the one who comes up with the name Tab Hunter. Coming highly recommended, Willson's most successful client is Rock Hudson, formerly an awkward truck driver with the unglamorous name Roy Scherer. Willson is well-known for spotting potential in actors, whereby looks and sex appeal are more important than talent. Acting, he thinks, could be learned as they go along. He invests in Hunter as a commodity which soon pays off. He succeeds in bringing about a 7-year contract with Warner Brothers.

Henry, whose chart displays a powerful Uranus/Neptune opposition, sits with his Uranus right on Tab's Saturn, which ignites the base of Tab's kite. Ambition meets manipulation. Also, the agent's Neptune sits at the top of Tab's kite in conjunction with the young actor's Sun/Pluto. It is the start of creating the illusion that Hunter will become the most attractive bachelor for millions of female fans. Another significant pairing is the agent's Saturn in conjunction with Tab's Moon/Chiron in the 12th. Saturn might give the Moon some safety, but also further its anxiety.

Property of Warner Bros
Under the old Hollywood studio system, which by the 1950s is slowly dying out, contract actors are literally their property. They mould them into stars, with images to create the perfect illusion for the movie magazines. Being owned by a company by contract and owing them one's livelihood is a strong 8th house analogy. After all, a contract actor is a product, and the studio wants to sell this product according to the needs of the moviegoing public. Hunter, with his wholesome, photogenic face, athletic body and blond, blue-eyed California surfer looks, is a very bankable product for Warner Brothers. They label him as the 'Sigh Guy', 'Swoon Bait', 'All-American Boy'; 'Boy Next Door' or 'Hollywood's Most Eligible Bachelor.' And the formerly shy Art Gelien transforms into a star who won't, as any good workhorse knows, bite the hand that feeds him. He gets cocky and soon he wants the keys to the kingdom, receiving top-billing next to the likes of Gary Cooper, Rita Hayworth or Sophia Loren.

Confidential **magazine**
Hunter is restless and looks for better opportunities, feeling type-cast. He decides to leave his Svengali Willson to work with another agent. A fatal step, as it soon turns out. To take revenge, Willson feeds *Confidential*

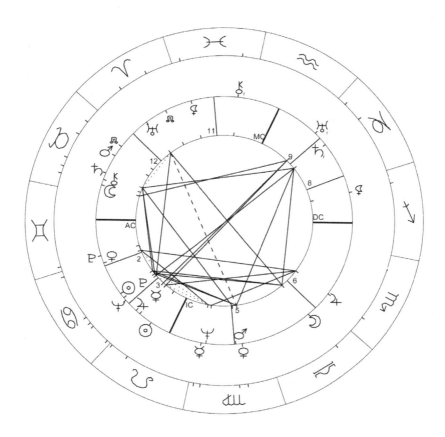

Inner wheel: Tab Hunter, 11 July 1931, 03:00, New York
Outer wheel: Henry Willson, 31 July 1911, 12:00,
Lansdowne, Pennsylvania

magazine an old story of the young Tab getting arrested for attending a so-
called 'limp-wristed all male pyjama party' in 1950. It later transpires that
revenge wasn't Willson's only motive. The blood thirsty *Confidential* had
already sniffed out that the agent's most precious client, sex symbol Rock
Hudson, is gay. A much bigger scoop with the potential to totally crush
Hudson's career. What to do? Willson quickly marries off Hudson with
his private secretary and, in exchange for keeping the lid on this explosive
story, he feeds the magazine with the old Hunter story. Hunter panics.

After all, only very few close friends know about his sexuality. Jack Warner, of all people, comes to the rescue, reassuring his young star that what is today's news would be tomorrow's toilet paper, but the rumours about Hunter's sexuality won't go away that easily. Warner Brothers double their efforts to pair Hunter with glamorous female stars. The studio fuels the publicity machine by sending Hunter off on countless dates with glamorous starlets and female stars. One of his film partners, Natalie Wood, who had co-starred with legend James Dean in *Rebel Without a Cause*, is a regular. They both play along, secretly dating other people. After being photographed at the many social functions, they always part ways at the back door, both secretly having a date with a man. When their fans, who expect an engagement, grow impatient, the joke goes, '*Natalie Wood and Tab Wouldn't*'.

Not so very secret lovers

Tab Hunter dates quite a few men over the years. As he is a very passionate and talented ice skater, it is no wonder that he falls in love with professional figure skater Ronnie Robertson (1937 – 2000), who wins the 1956 Olympics. The two of them share their love for skating, a Neptunian sport, because gliding, spinning and jumping give the illusion of defying gravity and have a dreamlike, elegant appeal. Ronnie's Jupiter sits directly at Hunter's Saturn at the kite base. But as rumours begin to leak the two are forced to separate.

Anthony Perkins is the most famous and interesting of Tab Hunter's lovers. A complex and twisted personality, he rises to stardom at about the same time as Hunter. Their relationship, like that with Ronnie Robertson, is an open secret in Hollywood. Perkins, born 4 April 1932 in New York, without birth time, has a stellium in Aries, which includes the Sun and Uranus. His Taurus Venus at the critical degree of 29°32′ sits widely on Tab's Moon in the 12th. The introverted intellectual from the East Coast is by temperament the very opposite of Hunter, which might have been part of the attraction. They try to see each other as often as possible. However, when gossip gets out, they decide to go their separate ways. When Hunter's career goes downhill, Perkin's is at its peak with *'Psycho'* (1960). An interesting postscript is that Perkins undergoes therapy in order to turn himself into a heterosexual, marries and fathers two sons. He dies of AIDS in 1992.

The sweet ride is over

At the end of 1958 Hunter is at the top of his career. But in terms of money, however, he feels frustrated. His most prestigious and highest grossing films have all been produced by other studios, not Warner Brothers. Jack Warner loans his big star out for $75,000 to $150,000, while Hunter only receives his weekly contract salary of $3,000. Also, the films he is offered by the studio aren't to his liking. Uranus transits his IC by conjunction; he feels restless, pushing his talents further with more demanding roles. But Warner feels that the teenage idol should be milked a little longer.

In synastry, one can trace Jack Warner's Jupiter forming squares with Hunter's Sun/Pluto and Saturn, while his Neptune/Pluto conjunction sits directly at Hunter's ascendant. This combination perfectly explains that Warner is able to exploit Hunter's talent so brilliantly. And so far Hunter has always played along, a win-win situation. But it is very hard to ignore a Uranus shaking up one's IC. Something's got to give...

Uranus plays an important role in Tab's chart. The planet of distance and disruption forms the apex of a T-square with both Sun/Pluto and Saturn, while being quincunx to Mars in the 5th. When Uranus hits his IC by transit the feeling of restlessness and wanting to be free from his studio contract becomes really intense. He throws caution to the winds and seeks independence. So much for Uranus. But as so often happens with transits, they come in a pack and have their own little contradictory agendas, which can feel at times overwhelming.

While Uranus shakes the roots of the 4th house, Saturn enters the 8th house, slowly but steadily returning to its natal position. When Hunter asks Warner how much it would cost to buy himself free from the contract, the mogul wants the astronomical sum of $100,000. When Saturn travels through the 8th house, life often demands that we clear ourselves from debts. It is often a period during which the native feels treated unfairly and that one has to work very much harder. It is also a time during which the values of others might clash with our own values.

Saturn transits through Tab's 8th house from early 1959 till the end of 1961. This period of almost 3 years really puts him through the wringer. While at the beginning of the transit he is a big household name in Hollywood and everybody's darling, the end of the transit sees him out of favour and eating humble pie. Without the protection of Warner Brothers the press can attack him whenever they want. Also, working as a freelance actor is much more difficult than playing safe under a studio contract. Reality soon hits him hard. His films from now on are considerably less prestigious and lucrative. The studio replaces him with a lookalike, Troy Donahue, 5 years Hunter's junior and the new teenage idol. Also, his new TV project, *The Tab Hunter Show* flops. This is not only due to the quality of the scripts, but also because he becomes the victim of a media shitstorm.

One day he finds himself splattered all over the tabloids. Neighbours whose invite to dinner the overworked Hunter had turned down had been so angered by this refusal that they decided to take revenge by fabricating this story and selling it to *Confidential* magazine. The media have a field day. This family is feeding the media with a story about Hunter violently whipping his dog, Fritz. It's a bitter taste of how vulnerable and unprotected a freelance actor can be. Things would have been different had he remained under the shield of Warner Brothers and their publicity department. Soon he finds himself in court on account of criminal charges of cruelty against animals. Although he is cleared of the charges, the damage to his image is done for good. His TV show, which probably would have flopped anyway due to its bad scripts, seems doomed under his flawed image. He receives vile letters, one of them reads:

> *Dear Dog Beater,*
> *You are the lowest thing on the face of the earth, and if I had any*
> *say in the matter, you'd be six feet under it. I hope they give you*
> *the death penalty.*

Turning point

The 1960s and 70s see Tab appear in various films, TV shows and on stage, he is constantly busy. Theatre in particular, which involves hitting the road, is extremely demanding. To constantly live out of a suitcase, travelling across the country and often being alone in bleak hotel rooms after performing on stage takes its toll. In 1980, aged 49, he suffers a severe heart attack. Pluto forms a double square with natal Sun/Pluto and Saturn. To top this off, Pluto is in opposition with natal Uranus, which, in consequence, produces a grand cross in cardinal quality. T-squares and grand crosses in cardinal quality often bring on the danger of overdoing things and depleting one's health. Pluto rules the intercepted Scorpio in Hunter's 6th house of health.

He recovers, like a true Saturn in 8th house hero, and takes a leap of faith when John Waters, trash movie director, persuades him to play in the film *Polyester*, with drag queen Divine. This collaboration becomes a big break for Hunter, reviving his career. The 1980s see him involved in many more projects, but eventually he decides to retire from show business, preferring to stay with his partner at their ranch with his beloved horses and dogs, happy to be forgotten and cherishing a life of privacy.

Cathartic moment

At the time of the publication of his book, Neptune sits on Tab's MC and Lilith sits on his IC. Neptune both rules illusion and disillusion, and when paired with Lilith can bring up issues of emancipation with it. Getting the whole gay thing off his chest feels liberating. The public at large react with a lot of sympathy and applauds his courageous step. Transiting Saturn forms an invigorating sextile with Tab's ascendant, giving him a whole new self-confidence. But he would never have done it without his partner, Allan Glaser, whose stabilising influence had been like a tonic for the restless artist. Although being 28 years younger, with a Sun/Jupiter conjunction in Sagittarius, sitting right on Hunter's descendant, they seemed to be the perfect couple.

Dirty Data

There is a good reason for labelling astrological birth data with the so-called Rodden Rating, named after famous astrologer Lois Rodden (1928 – 2003). It prevents spreading astrological birth data which is not reliable. In the case of Tab Hunter I noticed too late that his birth time of 3:00am is taken out of his biography and falls under the Rodden Rating DD, which stands for dirty data. Now what to do? Erase this chapter from my book? I just couldn't do it. His story is captivating and very moving. It encapsulated nearly every facet of the 8th house. And of course I could argue that the way he was described by many of this contemporaries fits well with a Gemini rising. Although he certainly had a shy and private side, he was also a sociable man who was always curious to meet people of all stripes. He had many interests and was never content to do just one thing. He could sing, dance, ice-skate, loved dogs and horses, collected antiques and adored travelling. Also, one should take into account that he had a Sun/Pluto conjunction in an opposition with Saturn. This is a powerful alignment and might account for much of his troubled and often suppressed nature; opening up never came easy to him. The fact that his chart falls under dirty data somehow seems appropriate for a chapter in a book about the 8th house for me. Believe me, I just couldn't part with it, so for those of you who object to using this data, please bear with me, won't you?

4
Apocalyptic Times – The Long Shadow of the 3rd Reich

'Apocalypse' can also be translated as 'Doomsday', 'Armageddon' and 'The end of the world'. On a collective level, society experiences these apocalyptic times during dramatic events which befall people like a volcanic eruption. A vivid example is the period between 1933 and 1945, the era of National Socialism in Germany. Its aftereffects are still visible, not only on an architectural level (cities all over Europe had to be rebuilt after the bombing of WWII, which was started by Hitler), but also in documentaries, movies and TV series. Children learn about the horrors of the Third Reich in school. And for a long time it seemed that critical awareness and reflection made modern Germany extra-alert about the dangers of fascist, xenophobic, racist and homophobic tendencies in society. But since the rise of right-wing populist party AFD (Alternative for Germany), there has also been a growing tendency to reinterpret the years 1933 – 1945 and downplay them, making Germans into victims. And while the majority of Germans are appalled by this, there are still some who share this view. By 2020, in the Eastern part of Germany, the AFD recorded election results as high as 25%.

The post-war period, with the quickly and drastically changing political division into capitalism on one side of the Iron Curtain and communism on the other one, did not really allow for a thorough moral reappraisal. The Nuremberg trials tried to set an example, but the majority of the population were otherwise engaged by trying to survive and removing the debris. Furthermore, these trials were often perceived as retaliation rather than fair justice. People wanted a fresh start and to forget everything about the horrors of war. Those who truly wanted to work through and learn from the traumatic past were in a minority and often kept from asking too many questions. After all, the bulk of the former government stuff had to be reinstalled by the occupying powers in order to keep the country on its feet. And although they now worked in a democracy, many of them still functioned by the routines of blind dictatorship obedience, uncritical of their individual role in the past. When pictures of the liberated concentration camps were made visible for the public, the general reaction was: "We didn't know about it. Nobody saw anything." What's more, many had hardened inside and suffered from pity fatigue. After all, didn't the whole population endure hardship, and have a sad story to tell? Also, the vivid realism in the pictures and news reels from the camps were too much to bear, so many resorted to defence mechanisms such as suppression, denial, rationalization and projection. The common agreement was: "Let's pretend we were all victims of the times and now let's not blame each other but rather build up the country and start afresh". It took 20 years before the next generation demanded answers from their parents and grand-parents in the mid-1960s, under the Uranus/Pluto conjunction.

I have chosen a couple of interesting charts to shed some light on this time. The main protagonist is Adolf Eichmann, high ranking SS-leader, also known as 'organiser of the end solution'. After the war he managed to escape to Argentina, but was caught by Mossad, the Israeli secret service and brought to trial in Jerusalem in 1961, where he was sentenced to death. I have also included the charts of the national socialist party NSDAP (1920) and the newly founded Federal Republic of Germany (1949).

Adolf Eichmann - The Banality of Evil

The fearsome, word-and-thought-defying banality of evil.
Hannah Arendt in 'Eichmann in Jerusalem' (1963), ch. 15.

To the very last [at his trial], Eichmann appeared emotionless, a human iceberg. Only once did I see him show any expression other than injured innocence. Films of the concentration camps were being screened in the courtroom. The houselights were out, but from the control booth, on a monitor, I could see the close-up of Eichmann. As the corpses of Bergen-Belsen were bulldozed into their final pit, Eichmann, on camera, smiled.
Alan Rosenthal, 'Eichmann, Revisited' in 'The Jerusalem Post' (20 April 2011).

Caught at last

Jerusalem, 1961. As the whole world becomes familiar with pictures and film footage of Nazi criminal Adolf Eichmann on trial, the unanimous reaction is sheer amazement and disbelief. How is it possible that a mass murderer, a monster, a creature from hell, can look so utterly unremarkably plain? This inconspicuous, sallow, middle-aged man, who could be taken as a shop keeper or bank clerk, is supposed to be responsible for the deportation and extinction of millions of Jews? Why doesn't he look more obviously diabolical and sinister, where are the traces of icy coldness in his plain features? Writer and journalist Hannah Arendt, reporting about the trial, has a name for this puzzling paradox: the 'banality of evil'. Arendt has Chiron in the 8th house, square Mercury in Scorpio in the 5th. For her undramatic and non-sensational analysis of Eichmann's personality she gets heavily criticised

Eichmann, 53 years of age, had been in hiding with his wife and children over the last 10 years in Argentina, under an assumed name and

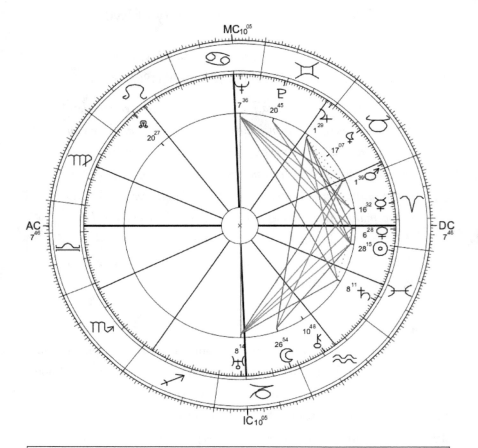

Adolf Eichmann, 19 March 1906, 17:30 MET, Solingen, Germany, RR:AA

8th house constellations

- Mars in Taurus at 8th house cusp as ruler of 2nd (Scorpio) and 7th (Aries) houses
- Mars sextile Neptune at MC and trine Uranus at IC
- Venus as ruler of 8th in Aries at descendant, square Uranus (at IC), square Neptune (at MC), Venus as apex of T-square
- Mars and Venus in mutual reception, both being in their signs of detriment

living mostly from low-paying jobs. A more dramatic contrast to his former flashy and important life in Germany, when he enjoyed the intoxicating sensation of power, could hardly be imagined. After 1945 he falls from grace into poverty and insignificance, a fugitive, eventually managing to escape to South America. This doesn't mean, however, that Nazi hunters have given up on him. Particularly tenacious is concentration camp survivor Simon Wiesenthal, who stays glued to Eichmann's heels. It is Wiesenthal's holy mission to bring Eichmann, one of the last remaining high-profile Nazis, the 'architect of the end solution', to justice. And he succeeds. Against all odds, Mossad contrives to catch him and bring him to justice in Israel, after Germany refuses to have him. It is one of history's bitter-sweet anecdotes that he ends up in Israel, the state which would never have existed in the first place if Eichmann had had his way, because there wouldn't have been any Jews left.

'The little Jew'

Adolf Eichmann grows up in the smallish city of Linz, in Austria. The family is very poor. His mother dies when he is still very young; his father, a simple, uneducated man, has to marry again to make ends meet, and unfortunately he chooses a woman who turns out to be the proverbial evil stepmother. She simply cannot bring herself to feel any affection for the awkward and sensitive boy. He is shy and an outsider; the other kids won't include him in their games. They bully him, calling him 'little Jew', on account of his hook nose, which is associated with Jews. Antisemitism is not uncommon in the early 20th century. Later, the Fascists don't really have to start, but rather build on long existing widespread prejudices. Jews are believed to be greedy, insidious and cunning. Adolf is not doing well in school; teachers tell him that he is too stupid to learn. These experiences of threefold rejection from stepmother, peers and teachers leave deep wounds in his self-esteem. He has to drop out of school and struggles along with low-paid jobs.

Birth of a human machine

Then suddenly, aged 18, the tide turns. He meets some young men who persuade him to join their organization; the 'Frontkämpfervereinigung Deutsch-Österreich' (German-Austrian front line fighters). The physically frail Adolf admires these tough guys in uniforms, self-confident and goal-oriented. They are out on a mission: to show the world Arian supremacy. He feels this is his chance to show everyone what a winner he can be. In 1932 he joins the NSDAP where he trains with the SS, the paramilitary and security organization and moves to Berlin.

Now his real talents come to the fore. It turns out that he possesses a unique meticulousness, a real devotion to serve and making himself useful. He is a clever organizer, able to see a problem in all its complexity as well as in the details. From 1935 on, the year of the 'Nuremberg Racial Laws', he is in charge of the 'Jewish' department, which has the mission to 'remove the harmful ethnic group from the German Reich'. In plain language this means dealing with the 'end solution', the mass extinction of all Jews. The party entrusts Eichmann with more and more responsibility. He sets up the 'Central Office for Jewish Emigration', with headquarters in Berlin, Vienna and Prague. All Jews are recorded, stripped of their valuables and transferred into ghettos. From now on there is no escape from the merciless extinction machinery. From 1941 on, Jews are forbidden to emigrate and the mass transport of over six million Jews to the concentration camps is set in motion. Eichmann has constructed a net of transport veins, trains and camps; a stroke of devilish genius. It is important to note that Eichmann doesn't just work from his desk, but actually visits various concentration camps where he witnesses mass shootings.

While his chart is strong in the cardinal and mutable cross, it lacks fixed quality. This means that the native can show a lot of initiative, while being able to flexibly adapt his actions to any sort of situation. A lack of fixed quality often signifies that the native does not know how to give processes and ideas enough time to properly ripen. There might also be a marked lack of inner calmness and too much aimless and restless activity. The Sun is in changeable Pisces in the 6th, the house of service. Planets in Pisces can give us a hard time when we want to get to the bottom of their motivation, since they tend to hide between other placements in the charts which are easier to grasp. Pisces is a dual sign. While one fish pulls on his side of the umbilical cord, trying to stay in this world, the counterpart pulls away to other worlds, yearning to dissolve altogether. Neptune, ruler of the 6th, is placed directly at the MC, a typical combination for anyone who wants to be of service for a higher cause. The native seeks to commit himself to something which he can idealise. Since this is the world of Neptune/Pisces, there is an unconscious current at work, a willingness to sacrifice and bend the truth. In order to climb the social ladder, Eichmann offers himself as henchman to a cause which seems superior to him. The Sun rules the 11th, the house of groups, organisations and like-minded spirits. In his case, the National Socialist German Workers' Party (NSDAP).

At long last, Eichmann isn't a misfit anymore; he feels like one of the few chosen ones as his fellow party members appreciate his special organising talents. Gone are the childhood days of humiliation, when kids called him 'little Jew'. From now on, he is part of a selected *Herrenrasse* (master race) with uber-ambitious goals, namely, to conquer new land in the east to secure ample space for the ever-growing superior Arian race. This is very much in line with a Taurus Mars in the 8th. While Taurus is about incorporation and collecting values and land, Mars in this sign works slowly and is driven by material interests. In the 8th, this placement works like a steam locomotive which may need a lot of time to get started, but is then almost unstoppable. The 8th house is about the values of others, in this case the possessions of the Jews. Mars as ruler of the 7th (encounters, public) and 2nd (own values and talents) in the secretive 8th house becomes entangled in the cruel intention to strip the Jews of their assets, and ultimately, their lives. This is, according to the party, a sort of expurgation to keep the Arian race pure and unspoilt, so that they will eventually rule the world.

Mars as ruler of the 7th house in the 8th also has a decidedly sexual connotation, especially in sensuous Taurus. Eichmann was married but had several affairs. When the ruler of the 7th (encounters) is in the 8th (intimacy, sex) there is a strong need to manipulate other people. Since the 7th is also the public and open enemies, another motivation is also to transform the values of others (8th). The total lack of affection and appreciation as a child leaves an enormous need for control and belonging.

Mars is connected by trine with Uranus at the IC. This indicates how detached from his own feelings Eichmann remains deep down. Perversely, this makes it easier (trine) for him to rob and kill millions of people without feeling at all guilty. Drastic changes during childhood (Uranus IC) can have the long-lasting effect of repressing pain to the point of feeling hardly anything. Mars also forms a sextile to Neptune at the MC, an indication that he is inspired (sextile) to serve an idealistic cause. Moon in Capricorn is in detriment and echoes the archetypical evil stepmother. It can be postulated that Eichmann wanted to take revenge on her, and the other children who called him 'little Jew', as well as his teachers who despaired of him. Of course, this sounds very simplistic and does not at all justify his actions, but it does make sense. Just think of Hitler and the grudge he held against the Vienna Academy of Arts who refused him as a student.

Venus, ruling the 8th house, is another key player in this chart. Aries gives her a fresh, cheeky, dynamic tint. In the 7th house she can enjoy herself by meeting other people. This social eagerness is also intensified by her very energetic position as apex of a cardinal T-square with Neptune at the MC and Uranus at the IC. This figure brings out an ambition to get on in life, no matter what. The Uranus/Neptune opposition may activate a propensity to become intoxicated with a mysterious, idealised image of one's vocation. The drive beneath this is the need to compensate for a childhood of radical upheavals and an inner tendency to cut off one's deepest feelings (Uranus IC). The MC is also associated with authority figures and official power structures. In Jerusalem, Eichmann's examiners are shocked to find that he doesn't show the slightest sign of remorse whatsoever. Instead, he plays down the significance of his own involvement in organising the transportation to the concentration camps. He simply claims that he was given orders by state authorities (MC); he sees himself as totally innocent (Neptune). He was just obeying orders and is thus not to be held accountable for any of the consequences. Pluto is in the 9th and rules the 2nd house. His own talents and values (2nd), are triggered by an inner need to broaden his horizons - foreigners, religion and travelling (9th). These triggers come with a touch of dogmatic possessiveness (Pluto), which could also lodge itself in the unconscious and serve as a life safer in times of danger and hardship. Eichmann survives years and years as a fugitive until he finally finds a (supposedly) safe hideout. Impoverished and isolated, he stays true to his political convictions and fancies himself innocent, only having obeyed his superiors and done his duty.

Now, let's look at the chart of the National Socialist German Workers' Party (NSDAP), the party which, for Eichmann, holds a promise of salvation.

National Socialist German Workers' Party (NSDAP)

Seduction of the masses

The occasion for the founding of the NSDAP is an evening on which Hitler holds one of his charismatic speeches at the Hofbräuhaus in Munich, an infamous hotspot for conservative nationalists. It is 1920, two years after the end of the First World War and Germany is on her knees. The humiliating Versailles treaty has forced Germany to accept full responsibility for the war and stripped her of about 10 percent of her land.

People are embittered because the treaty has created so much resentment. There are rumours that the German army had not really lost

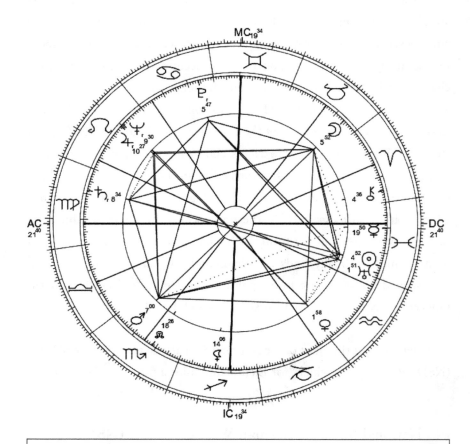

National Socialist German Workers' Party (NSDAP)
Foundation chart, 24 February 1920, 19:00 UT Munich, Germany

8th house constellations

- Kite with Moon at the tip in 8th as ruler of 11th
- Mars, ruler of 8th in 2nd
- Moon sextile Pluto in 10th, sextile Sun/Uranus in 6th
- Moon opposition Mars
- Moon square Jupiter/Neptune in 11th
- Moon square Venus in 5th

the war, but had been betrayed by certain politicians, who by negotiating an unnecessary surrender stabbed the army in the back.

After the abdication of Kaiser Wilhelm, the post-war German Reich is a republic and no longer a monarchy. But politicians and population are inexperienced with this form of state and government. The election system, unlike in Germany after 1949, does not operate a 5 percent hurdle, so any small party can be elected into parliament, which will eventually become a dangerous, predetermined breaking-point and source of chaos.

Adolf Hitler (Neptune and Pluto in the 8th) uses his magnetic charisma and strong personality to build up his new party with a simple combination of xenophobia, victimisation and national pride. This appeals to the humiliated and desperate working class, the main losers of the war. The chart is a firework of aspect figures with a marked 8th house and the Moon at the tip of a kite. The Moon in a party chart represents the party members and voters. The 8th is the house of debts, but also manipulation, taboo, secret police and neurotic fixations. Historians claim that many of the later voters of 1933 were actually in the dark about the real motives of the NSDAP. Those who voted for them allegedly mainly wanted a strong leader to manoeuvre the country through the depression and help Germany to rise again from the ashes. The Moon at the apex of a kite of a party is a powerful emotional trigger for the electorate. We also need to factor in the Moon's sextile to Sun/Uranus in Pisces in the 6th, with the promise of full employment.

Hitler has a Moon/Jupiter conjunction in Capricorn in exact opposition to the party's Pluto. His Venus/Mars conjunction conjoins the party's Moon, which is in turn part of a fixed T-square with Mars in Scorpio in the 2nd, and squares Venus in the 5th and Jupiter/Neptune in the 11th. One might say Hitler serves as the focal point for illusion and idealisation of German society.

The Moon in the 8th rules in the 11th, the house of like-minded spirits. The ruler of the 8th, in turn, is Mars in Scorpio in the 2nd house,

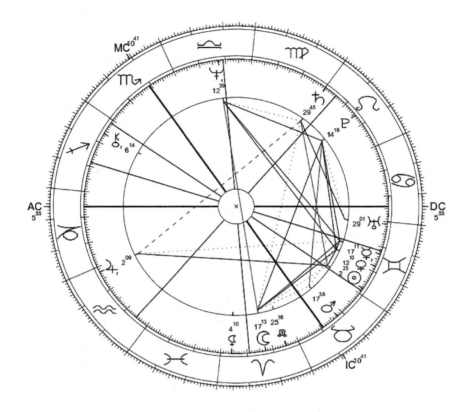

Formation of Federal Republic of Germany 25 May 1949, 00:00,
Bonn, Germany

8th house constellations

- Saturn as ascendant ruler in 8th at the critical degree of 29° Leo
- Saturn sextile Uranus
- Sun ruler of 8th in 5th, opposition Chiron in 11th
- Sun trine Jupiter in 1st

the values of others are transferred into the party's own values. The capacity for mass manipulation can be attributed to Pisces Mercury as ascendant ruler at the descendant, supported by a grand trine in water with Sun/ Uranus, Mars and Pluto. Pluto rules the 3rd house of marketing and public relations, areas in which the Nazis excel, just think of the newspaper party machine *The Folk Observer* (Völkischer Beobachter) and later in the 1930s, the newsreels.

Eichmann's Sun in Pisces in the 6th perfectly echoes the party's chart, the common denominator being to serve a higher purpose. The NSDAP chart has a good portion of fixed quality, thus being able to compensate Eichmann's lack in that department. Also, Eichmann's MC is conjoined with the party's Pluto, and his Chiron forms a trine to the party's Pluto.

A Fresh Start with a Guilty Conscience: Federal Republic of Germany (1949)

Unfinished business

The national chart for the newly founded Federal Republic of Germany has Capricorn rising and Moon in Aries, which is very apt for a nation which has to find new structures (Capricorn) and to start from scratch (Aries). Saturn in the 8th, moreover, signifies a heavy burden of guilt and debt. The Sun, ruler of the 8th, is in the 5th, which implies that national pride must be re-established and that one must show the world that Germany will strive to become a major player again. The majority of the people are of one mind, following the motto: 'Remove the ruins and forget the horrors of the past'. Sun trine Jupiter signifies a veritable economic miracle ('Wirtschaftswunder') - as it turns out, no other country in Europe will emerge so quickly from the ruins of WWII. In stark contrast, countries which won the war, like the UK, suffer from food rationing until as late as 1954.

The Sun is in the 5th house. Its trine to Jupiter is a jolly carefree affair, one might guess. It might even feel a bit too cocksure about its own strength. On the other hand, it is also the ruler of the 8th, which contains Saturn. With this extra luggage, the Sun might feel the burden of responsibility and adheres to the rule of 'just roll up your sleeves and get it done'. The Sun is also in opposition to Chiron in Sagittarius in the 11th, which must reflect on the Sun's self-esteem, in practice, the identity pattern of post-war Germans. Saturn in the 8th often manifests as a guilty conscience. Chiron in the 11th signifies a collective wound inside society as a whole. Chiron wounds don't show themselves too obviously, but rather tend to be patched up by their owner, so that nobody will see it. After all, wounds can be a source of shame. Especially where the luminaries are concerned, Chiron can feel very uncomfortable. Rebuilding a country and pretending that nothing has happened can be a way of patching up a Chiron wound. This placement might account for the fact that so many post-war Germans resort to all kinds of defence mechanisms. The 12 'Nazi' years are best swept under the carpet; collectively denied, suppressed, relativized and even reinterpreted.

In 1949 the other new German state is also founded, and it is of some significance that the DDR (German Democratic Republic) has Saturn in the 8th as well. By this time the Cold War is already full on. Old enemies have become allies, while new enemies behind the Iron Curtain endanger the delicate peace in Europe. West Germany is a vital military stronghold against communism. Therefore, it must by all means be brought back on its feet as soon as possible, helped by the famous Marshall plan.

How culprits and hangers-on turn into victims
The Nuremberg trials (1945 – 1946), the historical revision of the Nazi past, try to set a moral example for the German people. Prominent Nazi henchmen are convicted, some with capital punishment. But there are also many acquittals. Moreover, hundreds or even thousands of influential

fascists escape after the war and disappear into hiding, many with new identities. The reason why so many can get away is that there is a closely-knit and very effective system of rope teams and sympathisers at work. After all, they all are in the same boat, each being a threat to the others by way of possible denunciation. Everyone can give compromising information about someone.

What's more, the majority of the population see the events before and during the war in quite a different light. The German people have just been overwhelmed by Hitler. Now, the years of occupation are experienced as degrading and humiliating; the Nuremberg trials are for many not justice, but acts of revenge and retaliation by the victors. There is simply no insight or moral revision by way of accepting responsibility on individual or social level as a nation. Why, after all these years of suffering, should anyone feel guilty? After all, the Germans suffered just as much, if not more so, from the bombing and starvation as every other nation. Wasn't it punishment enough that the cities were in ruins and millions had died?

Let sleeping dogs lie

The young nation borders the new deadly enemy, the Communist bloc, and needs to get back to normal as soon as possible. Since there are no alternatives, the allies have to take on the bulk of the former official apparatus with civil servants, policemen and judicial officers from the Third Reich. A paradoxical situation: while officially the new Germany is a democracy, the people in charge are nearly all former fascists. The most notorious example is the renowned lawyer Hans Globke, close confidant to chancellor Konrad Adenauer (Jupiter in the 8th as part of a grand cross in fixed quality). Globke was involved in setting up the Nuremberg Racial Laws of 1935. With a man like him as high up in power, there is of course only very limited interest in tracking down members of the former Nazi elite to bring them to justice. And so the common consensus is to let sleeping dogs lie. Better to concentrate on the future, which will be brighter than the past.

The Federal Intelligence Service has been in the know about the whereabouts of Adolf Eichman for quite a long time. Nevertheless, there doesn't seem to be too much pressure to become more active in this matter – it's too hot a topic. In Frankfurt, Fritz Bauer, a Jewish lawyer who has been on Eichmann's track since the war, forwards this crucial piece of information to the Mossad, the secret service in Israel, hoping to galvanise them into action. He hopes that Israel will catch him and bring him to justice. Eichmann is arrested in Argentina on 11 May 1961 and taken secretly to Israel. The trial, transmitted by radio and television, receives huge public interest all over the world. 16 years after the war the whole world learns in detail about the horrors of the Holocaust, and with it, the people of Israel. Here, there had been much mistrust and ambivalence against the survivors of the concentration camps. Even President Ben Gurion is of two minds in this matter. After all, he has much to gain in keeping a friendly relationship with Germany, which supports Israel generously (out of guilty conscience), but the trial cannot be stopped. The verdict is unanimous. After months and months of waiting the judgement is enforced on 1 June, 1962. Mars transits Eichmann's 8th house. The ashes are thrown into the sea.

5
Entanglements

Crises can materialise in the form of dramatic entanglements. We might find ourselves caught up in complicated situations with no easy way out. The 8th house, more than any other place in the chart, is associated with entanglements, and can indeed hold serious troubles in store. These might arise through power games, boundary crossings, or dealing with taboos. Maybe we don't see the writing on the wall until we actually hit it. Or we can't imagine how a situation could turn from promising to disastrous.

We may find ourselves attracted to people who turn out to be clingy and manipulative. We might experience dark facets of our own psyche which have been hidden before. What strikes me as particularly interesting here is the fact that in this house it is almost impossible to differentiate between good and evil, black and white, hero and villain. As a matter of fact, things are more often than not muddled and mixed up.

The deeply entangled and ambivalent relationship between Kaiser Wilhelm II and his English mother Vicky is a vivid example. While his love for her became almost obsessive, her feelings for him were deeply tainted by guilt and shame. Over the years they drifted further and further apart, until they became completely estranged. Even though history has proven that Wilhelm II played an important role in plunging Europe in the abyss of WWI and we only see him as a narcissistic, teutonic monster, there is another side to him. He was a deeply troubled and lonely little boy and had to endure unimaginable horrific treatments for his withered arm. Vicky on the other hand was torn between her natural altruistic feelings of a mother and her guilt at not having produced a perfectly healthy heir to the throne.

Another pertinent example of a fatal entanglement is that of famous gay writer Truman Capote and murderer Perry Smith. Capote embarked on digging as deeply as possible into the background story of the gruesome homicide of an innocent country family in Kansas, in which Smith was involved. During the research, which also involved interviews with convicts Smith and his partner in crime, Hickock, Capote became close with Smith, too close. Their relationship was highly passionate and involved sympathy as well as mistrust and frustration. The book which Capote wrote about this case took several years, because the actual execution of Smith was delayed several times. *In Cold Blood* was an unapparelled success at the time, but Capote was so drained that he never wrote another hit.

In Cold Blood

Truman Capote's non-fiction novel, a true story of bloody murder in rural Kansas opens a window on the dark underbelly of post-war America.
'The Guardian', ranking 'In Cold Blood' at number 84 of the 100 best novels

No one will ever know what In Cold Blood *took out of me. It scraped me right down to the marrow of my bones. It nearly killed me. I think, in a way, it did kill me.*
Truman Capote (1924 – 1984)

America is innocent no longer
15th November, 1959. In the early morning hours, four single gun shots sound from the Clutter home of Holcomb, Kansas. The Clutter family - Herb, his wife Bonnie and their children, Nancy and Kenyon, have been most brutally murdered. This crime is like no other in the state's history. An entire family killed for no apparent motive; culprits unknown. Kansas, a typical mid-western state, is a region of friendly, God-fearing people,

known for its vast plains, and probably the safest place in America. Kansans are people who trust one another and don't lock their doors. A massacre like this in New York or Los Angeles would have been expected, but in Kansas? This incident shakes the very foundation of trust, not only in Kansas, but all over the country. The heartland of America is innocent no longer. Until the culprits are caught, the citizens of Holcomb have all kinds of ideas about who committed the crime, which is truly scary. Who knows? Maybe the murderers are someone in their very midst? Paranoia, for the first time, grips Kansans. The Clutters had been an admired family and the least likely candidates to be murder victims. Herb Clutter was a Kansas success story; a wealthy farmer, college educated, a pillar of the community. President Eisenhower had selected him to serve on the Federal Farmer Credit Board. And although the Clutters were well-to-do, they never kept a lot of cash in the house, so what is the motive?

A much, much bigger story...

A short article about the crime appears in the *New York Times*, which catches the attention of celebrated author Truman Capote (*Breakfast at Tiffany's*). A total sucker for crime, he is instantly intrigued by the story, as well as the urban setting. Kansas is as far away as possible from his glamorous and sophisticated New York lifestyle; a strangely foreign world worthy of exploration. He wants to write an article for the magazine *The New Yorker* about the impact of such a heinous crime on a small sheltered community. Accompanied by his childhood-friend, fellow author Nelle Harper Lee (*To Kill a Mockingbird*), he boards the train; a trip which will change his life and lead to his greatest success as well as his final downfall. Welcome to the rollercoaster of the 8th house.

The gay, eccentric and tiny Truman Capote (5ft 2in), is a sight which none of the Western Kansans has ever seen before. His effeminate mannerisms, high pitched voice and flamboyant way of dressing stands out strikingly in this conservative macho land, where men wear high heel cowboy boots with pointed toes and Stetson hats. He could just as easily be an alien from outer space, popping out of a flying saucer. But his friendly manners and entertaining personality, assisted by his friend Nelle, soon bring people to like him and open up. Eventually he even becomes the toast of the town and everyone wants to have him over for dinner. Just as Capote has finished his article and is about to return to New York, the culprits are captured on 30 December, following an extensive manhunt which had stretched as far as Mexico. This changes everything. He simply must stay to meet the murderers to find out everything about their motives, so he prolongs his visit. Little does he know that he will have to come back to Kansas again and again, for the next five years. At first he decides to stay detached, as any professional should. But after spending endless hours with the protagonists, making thousands of pages of notes, he gets more and more personally involved. He becomes attached to the murderers, even feeling sympathy, particularly for one of the two, Smith. This is totally against his will, but there is nothing he can do about it - it feels like being caught in a vortex. Soon he is sucked into the tragedy, and in the process turns what was originally only a very sad and disturbing piece of news into a major national tragedy. And he feels this has to become a book, with the makings of a bestseller.

The two culprits, 28-year-old Richard Eugene Hickock and 31-year-old Perry Smith, both have a history of petty crime, although neither of them has ever been involved in murder before. While serving time in Lancing penitentiary, Richard Eugene Hickock is told by a cellmate about Herb Clutter and his alleged home safe containing some ten thousand dollars. Hickock is obsessed by the idea of robbing this Clutter. After his release he contacts an old friend, Perry Smith. Smith is a drifter and a dreamer. They prove a deadly combination, because they agree that they will leave no witnesses alive. Hickock later repeatedly tries to pin the actual shootings on Smith, who in turn claims that he only accounted for the father and the boy, while Hickock shot the mother and the girl.

From a psychological viewpoint Hickock, although talkative and blessed with an uncanny memory for details, is rather exhausting and uninspiring. Smith, on the other hand, is in another league. His moods can change from whining self-pity to feeling utterly elated about some book or whim. While undoubtedly sly and cruel, he has also surprisingly sensitive and tender sides to him. Capote finds his sad eyes and melodic voice irresistible. What also makes him special is the fact that he is remarkably short, measuring only 5ft 2in, exactly like Capote. Soon they form a sort of friendship. Although, judging from the outside, the sophisticated and celebrated author and the white-trash criminal can't possibly have anything in common, there is an invisible bond: a deeply troubled and joyless childhood.

Abandonment
Smith: Ending up the wrong path
In the chart of Perry Smith, Mars and Pluto immediately jump out with their prominent placement in Cancer in the 8th house; being both the classical and modern collective ruler here. Mars is in a square with Uranus in the 4th house of childhood and home, which the planet of disruptions shares with the sensitive Moon. Since the Moon is also ruler of the 8th, these two water houses gain momentum. Transformative crises (8th) in childhood (4th), with many changes in living situations. The house in which the Moon is placed often indicates the area in life where we are most vulnerable and prone to experience intense fluctuation. Also interesting are the squares between Moon and Mars and Moon and Pluto, both indicative of a nervous, highly-strung, over-sensitive nature. Since the Moon in good-natured and optimistic Aries particularly depends on authentic and loving support from a mother-figure, these challenging aspects seem very harsh. Saturn in the 1st on the other hand often comes with a somewhat stoic outlook in life. One doesn't expect to get anything for free, but rather

has to work hard and be content with very little. The Moon also forms a trine with Saturn, a combination which supports the feeling of being able to deal with disappointments in life.

The Sun at 4° Scorpio in the 11th is in opposition to Jupiter/Chiron, which indicates a hyperbolic and at the same time wounded self-perception. The quincunx between Sun and Uranus supports the likelihood of a disruptive childhood as well as a certain general moodiness and unpredictable episodes of feeling detached from the world. On the other hand, we have a retrograde Mercury in art-loving Libra in a square with Pluto and Venus/Lilith rising, so there are also definitely softer, more feminine sides to consider. Pluto rules the 12th house, which is about fantasy, subconsciousness, but also about underhanded actions, detention and obstructing the truth.

Smith and his siblings suffer under their alcoholic and abusive mother, who leaves his father when the boy is 7 and who dies from choking on her own vomit when he is 13. After that he is put into a Catholic orphanage, where he is constantly punished for bed wetting, allegedly a result of malnutrition. There is also an incident in another orphanage where one of the caretakers tries to drown him. Later he reunites with his father. The two of them try to live an itinerant existence, travelling across the country, barely making ends meet and constantly quarrelling. Eventually Smith goes off the rails, joins a street gang and gets mixed up in various petty crimes, finally ending in juvenile detention. A tendency for suicide runs in the family; Smith's father takes his own life, aged 92, as do two of Smith's siblings. He himself is almost killed in a motorcycle accident; both legs are horribly shattered and only badly patched up, causing him constant pain and leading him to becoming addicted to Aspirin. To overcompensate for his childlike height, he lifts dumbbells, resulting in a thick, crouching torso, which looks somewhat over-sized, especially against his skinny legs and tiny girl feet. He also has quite elaborate tattoos all over his arms. Living inside his own fantasy world, he likes to look in the mirror all the time, a narcissistic need for reassurance, often found with neglected

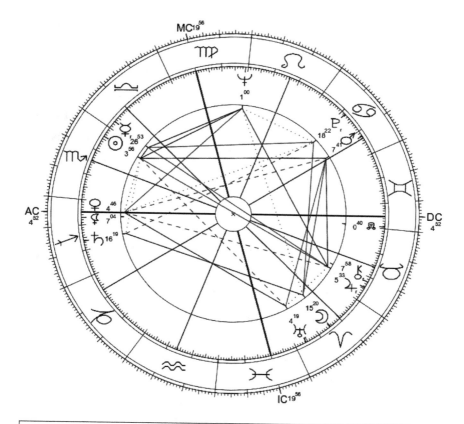

Perry Smith, 27 October 1928, 09:30 EST, Huntingdon, West Virginia, RR:AA

8th house constellations

- Mars and Pluto in 8th
- Pluto ruler of 12th
- Mars ruler of 5th
- Moon, ruler of 8th, in 4th, square Pluto
- Pluto square Mercury in 11th and quincunx Saturn in 1st

children who have no clue who they are and what makes them loveable.

Capote's Moon, conjunct Saturn, sits at 4° Scorpio, exactly on Smith's Sun. Luminary conjunctions in synastry are an indication for a strong bond, albeit not necessarily without ambivalence, especially when Saturn plays its part as well. Capote is a kind of mentor/friend for Smith and wields a huge influence on how the criminal grows to define his own identity (Sun). Capote, on the other hand, feels a deep bond (Moon), but also a guilty conscience (Saturn).

Capote: Escape to fame
Like Smith, Capote is also haunted by his lonely and melancholy boyhood. His real name, under which he lived the first years of his life, indicates the presence (or rather, absence) of a father figure: Truman Streckfuss Persons. His mother Lilli Mae is just 17 when she meets and marries the charming and ambitious salesman, Arch Persons, in a small town in Alabama. Shortly after little Truman is born it becomes increasingly clear that the marriage is in trouble. Lilli Mae wants more out of life and attempts to realise her dreams from a series of fly-by-night lovers, a lifestyle which is ill-suited to a little boy. Truman is left with babysitters or locked up for the night in a hotel room, his cries left unanswered. He often waits up the whole night until his parents eventually return, each time fearing that they might never come back at all and have just abandoned him. When he's just six years old they leave him for good and dump him with three old spinster aunts. They live in a strange, highly organized and very religious household, leading a monotonously rigid existence. Since everyone is constantly bickering there is a lot of tension in the air. Although not exactly a happy life for young Truman, it is however the source of his interest in studying human nature and storytelling. In the evenings all the neighbours would assemble on the porch, telling strange sad stories of human tragedies, ghosts and inexplicable phenomena. To fill his many lonely hours he teaches himself to read and write, which soon becomes his whole world. He is fascinated by stories and

details and can never get enough of them, carrying his notepad wherever he goes. Unlike other children he never wants to play, preferring instead to spend many hours each day after school writing, like an obsession. At age eleven, he wins a children's writing contest. There is no doubt he has talent.

Then his mother turns up out of the blue and takes him with her to exciting New York where her husband, José García Capote, a rich bookkeeper, adopts him. But the new father figure soon disappears again, convicted for embezzlement. Sun in the 8th house...

Fame comes to Truman at the young age of 24 when his first novel *Other Voices, Other Rooms* is published and is an instant success. Its Southern Gothic style and atmosphere of isolation and decay has strong autobiographical traits. It is mostly about a son's search for his father.

Capote has Sun in the 8th in Libra, an odd combination of a diplomatic, harmony-loving sign and a house of border-crossing, trouble and crisis. The square with Pluto at the cusp of the 6th house indicates a tendency to become obsessive. For him, from childhood on, there are no shades of grey, but only the two extremes of being either totally consumed (with work, love, society, drugs) or completely detached and indifferent. Since the Sun is involved, it involves both his journey into self-discovery and his perception of an (inner) father figure. Mercury, ruler of the 8th, in Virgo, is the only earth placement in his chart, thus of some significance. The great astrologer, Richard Idemon, called these placements 'singletons'. Mercury sits on the 8th house cusp, which means that both motives and actions meet here, without any detours or roundabouts involving other houses. Mercury in Virgo is razor sharp and witty; a brilliant observer and stickler for details. The opposition with Uranus on the 2nd house cusp suggests that the native needs to distance himself from time to time in order not to get sucked too deeply into drama. This is maybe Capote's biggest challenge. The Sun rules the descendant and brings a need for social interaction into the 8th. He is very keen on gossip and known to be

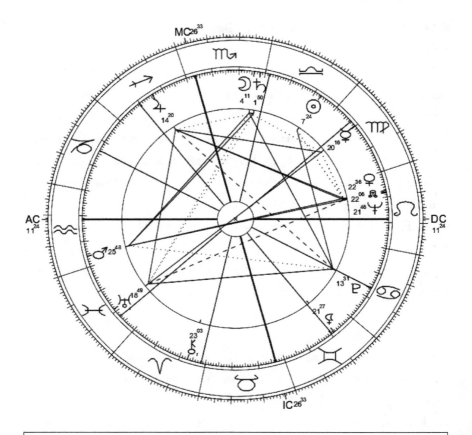

Truman Capote, 30 September 1924, 15:00 CST New Orleans, Louisiana, RR:B

8th house constellations
- Sun in 8th as ruler of 10th
- Sun square Pluto on cusp of 6th
- Ruler of 8th, Mercury, on cusp of 8th, as part of T-square with Jupiter and Uranus

a good listener, being entrusted with many intimate secrets by his friends. Unfortunately, he cannot always keep these to himself. When, in the 1970s he spills the beans about his New York society ladies, movie star friends and writer colleagues, he is punished very hard by many of them who turn away from him for good. His Sun is in opposition to Smith's Uranus, the signifier of a classic closeness-distance conflict. Since Mars is square Smith's Uranus, there is also a contradiction between being both passionately involved (Mars) and feeling alienated (Uranus). The Moon/Saturn conjunction, which is arguably one of the most challenging aspects one can find, is trine Pluto in the 6th, thus offering an escape from feeling lonely and abandoned by hard and dedicated work. His dramatic, artistic side is indicated by Venus/Neptune in Leo on the North Node in the 7th, in a passionate opposition with Mars in Aquarius in the 1st.

On death row

The trial in March 1960 ends, as expected, with the death sentence, which in Kansas is execution by hanging. However, due to successive appeals over the next few years the judgement isn't enforced until 14 May 1965. During this time Truman Capote writes *In Cold Blood*, which naturally wouldn't have a proper ending before the final fate of the two murderers is eventually decided. In consequence, this means that he is left in limbo for five long years, experiencing a roller coaster of hope and agony.

Likewise, Smith and Hickock, who from 1963 onwards live on death row under the most reduced circumstances, having to wait out their final fate, gradually become more and more desperate and hopeless.

Smith's and Hickock's letters to Capote number in the hundreds, and give a vivid testimony of life on death row. Capote becomes the chief focus of their lives, but Smith always claims that he takes priority over Hickock in Capote's affection and is probably right.

The Capote-Smith composite (reference place method) is charged with ambivalence and tension. Neptune, the planet of deception and longing for peace, acts as a key player at the tip of a striking yod figure in the 8th, involving quincunxes with Mars/Chiron in the 4th and the Moon in the 1st, as well as an opposition with chart ruler Jupiter in the 2nd. A yod is a signifier for a tendency to feel torn apart, nervous and being caught between three different places. It's like trying to sit on a wobbly chair with just three legs. Between 1960 and 1965 Capote finds it hard to stay in Kansas for too long. He feels restless and overwhelmed by the situation, as well as guilty and useless. It's hard to accept his feelings of sympathy and pity for Smith, he is a murderer after all. They are both stuck with each other, each having taken possession over the other. Until Capote's death in 1984, his fate is inescapably intertwined with Smith's.

Smith lives for Capote's letters and for everything he sends into his dim cell; books, magazines, photographs. Neptune rules the 3rd, the house of communication and seeks cross-border merging in the 8th. Unfortunately, this is inevitably frustrated by the rather toughened-up Moon in Capricorn in the 1st and the distant and unreliable Uranus in the 3rd. The placement of the yod in the 1st (Moon), 3rd (Uranus) and 8th (Neptune) houses captures the great pressure under which both of them suffer. While none of Capote's letters have survived, those from Smith to the author have. They often express his tender feelings for Capote. A photograph with Capote and his dog brings Smith to tears.

> "I cannot believe that I have ever seen a more pleasing and
> contented expression (on Capote's face) – it appears to have
> an effect on me similar to an anodyne and it would be useless
> for you to ask me to return it."

The Moon in Capricorn often indicates difficulties with being emotionally at ease and sharing tender feelings. There are many times when Capote can hardly bear the feeling of ambivalence between longing to be freed at last by their execution and suffering from a terribly guilty conscience of using the two young men. On the other hand, they had committed a heinous

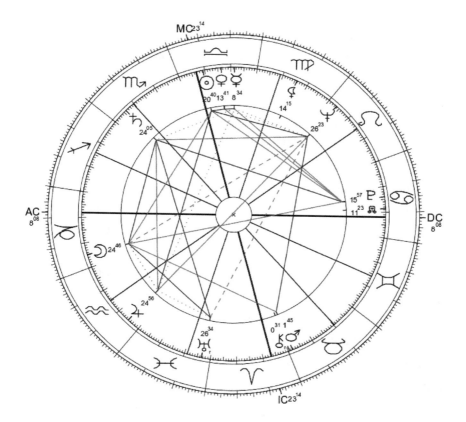

Composite Smith/Capote

8th house constellations

- Neptune in 8th as ruler of 3rd
- Neptune apex of yod with Moon and Uranus
- Neptune square Saturn
- Neptune trine Mars/Chiron
- Neptune opposition Jupiter
- Neptune sextile Sun at MC

crime and cold-bloodedly killed four innocent people. Don't they deserve to pay with their own lives for this? Jupiter in the 2nd opposite Neptune in the 8th brings out a manipulative streak in both partners, albeit presumably unintentionally. Each one becomes a victim of his own hidden agenda, which makes it hard to trust, at some point even resulting in paranoia. There is a source of contention which is projected on to the other person causing problems in following through, where intentions can be foiled by an inability to realise them. And sadly, at the end of the day, they will never be completed in a satisfactory way. The T-square with Saturn as apex additionally emphasizes the issue of 'painful sacrifices' in the 11th (friendship).

Capote is present at the execution, an experience which will haunt him for the rest of his life. At least he can publish his book, which turns out to be a major bestseller. But the book is a mixed blessing. While it earns him millions of dollars, it also plunges him into bouts of depression and despair. He takes to alcohol and drugs, which only worsens his condition and causes serious episodes of hallucinations. He can never pick up on the success of *In Cold Blood*. After publishing a tell-it-all book about his glamorous society friends, he finds himself alone and defeated. He dies in 1984, shortly before his 60th birthday.

A Royal Tragedy

Placements in the 8th often determine all kinds of intense encounters and passions. The relationship between Kaiser Wilhelm II (1859 – 1941) and his mother Vicky, later called 'Empress Friedrich' (1840 – 1901), both with prominent 8th house placements, is a gripping example. It illustrates perfectly how love can turn into hatred, and competitiveness can serve as over-compensation for narcissistic distresses, even to the point of war.

The taboo of a crippled prince

Potsdam, 27 January, 1859. Vicky, the 19-year-old Prussian crown princess, eldest daughter of Queen Victoria and her German husband Prince Albert of Saxe-Coburg and Gotha, has been in labour for many agonising hours. The baby is in breech position, at that time and age an almost fatal situation. The young woman has been given chloroform in order to alleviate the pain. Queen Victoria, who herself had been confined after giving birth to her ninth child only two years earlier, swears by this wonder drug. But the newly-discovered anaesthetic is still not fully understood, and surgeons don't quite have the hang of dosing it. In this case, they overdid it and used far too much: Vicky feels almost numb and can't push properly.

What to do? After a long debate, one brave British doctor reaches inside the royal uterus to turn the baby into the correct position and the boy is at last safely delivered. What a relief, it's a healthy male heir for Prussia. But after a couple of days the nurse notices that the baby's left arm doesn't move. Something is clearly amiss. The surgeon must have grasped the left shoulder too tightly, thereby badly injuring the arm nerve tissue. This condition, called Erb's palsy, leaves the child forever handicapped, with a withered left arm about six inches shorter than his right.

The following months are a nightmare for Vicky and her husband Fritz. The young and inexperienced mother feels guilty, having failed in her duty to produce a healthy heir. An injured infant, a cripple, is an absolute taboo in deeply conservative German society. Prussia is a military state.

Any future leader of the country is expected to be decisive, confident and physically strong. A man's man, a warrior, a figure of authority. A prince with any kind of visible deformity is a nightmare scenario. In her daily letters to her mother, the Queen, she begs her to keep it a secret and not even tell her siblings. Vicky, with a will of iron (counselled by all the experts of the Prussian court) now sets a train of 'remedies' in motion, aimed to 'cure' the withered arm. The doctors are clueless and blame a weakness of the muscles instead of recognising that the nerve tissue is chronically damaged and incurable.

German medicine at that time was an odd mixture of medieval, superstitious treatments and modern science. The little boy was more-or-less a guinea pig, having to endure various absurd treatments. He had to place his arm inside a freshly slaughtered hare, so that the strength of the animal could be transferred into the arm. Also, he was exposed to electro-shocks, a state-of-the-art development in medicine, believed to be extremely efficient and stimulating. Since the adult Wilhelm was famous for his restlessness, extreme excitability and nervous fits, one can only assume that this treatment damaged his nervous system as well.

In order to force his lame arm to function, the doctors bound the healthy one behind his back, which of course made the toddler even more insecure. And it was only after ten years of torture that the royal family faced the bitter truth: there was no cure. Wilhelm, however, was psychologically scarred for the rest of his life, with dramatic results for the whole world, because he would indeed become Kaiser.

Fizzled ambitions of a perfect princess

Vicky's chart bursts with tension and high hopes. The first born, she was in many respects the most promising of Queen Victoria's and Prince Albert's nine children. To her serious and frugal father, to whom she was devoted (Moon/Moon conjunction in Scorpio), she was the perfect daughter, her character the result of his strict regime, a perfect little female 'mini-me'.

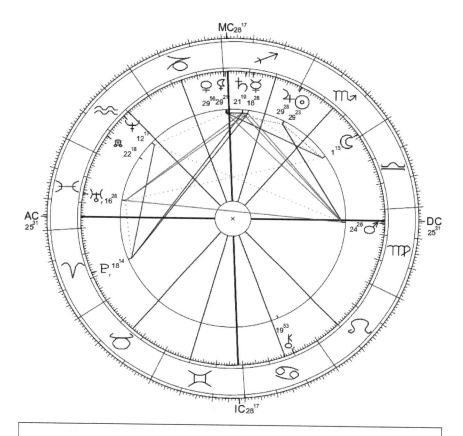

Frederica (Vicky), Empress of Germany, 21 November 1840, 13:50 LMT, London, RR:AA

8th house constellations

- Sun/Jupiter conjunction in 8th
- Sun/Jupiter sextile Mars
- Sun rules 6th, Jupiter rules 9th and 10th
- Pluto, ruler of 8th in 1st house, trine Mercury/Saturn in 9th and sextile Neptune in 12th

Her Scorpio Sun conjoins Jupiter at the critical 29°, a placement to which Frank Clifford attributes a certain inevitability and 'fatefulness'. Sun/Jupiter in a woman's chart can signify an idolised father/partner relationship. Vicky adored Albert, as she would later adore her German husband Friedrich. In the 8th, this placement can have a passionate and morbid touch and has a propensity to go to extremes.

Both father (age 42) and husband (age 56) would die prematurely, leaving her bereft of love and protection, but all the more clinging onto the memories of these men. Moon in Scorpio also mirrors her mother Queen Victoria's morbid 'Albert death cult' which every member of the family had to follow religiously. The 'Widow of Windsor' was an absolute control freak, holding a lifelong grip on her eldest daughter, demanding to be informed about every detail of her life. Over the years more than 30,000 letters were exchanged between mother and daughter, giving fascinating insights into a highly neurotic and ambivalent relationship.

Mercury conjunct Saturn in Sagittarius in the 9th constitutes an insatiable curiosity. A quick learner, alert, interested, accomplished and pretty, Vicky had many gifts and privileges. But, although bearing the title 'Princess Royal' from her first year, she was in truth still only a girl. Venus and Lilith sit right on the MC, again both at the very critical 29° in lofty and ambitious Sagittarius. In different times and circumstances, she could have excelled in many fields. Similarly, her mother Victoria was very young when it became apparent that she was the heir presumptive to succeed her uncle William IV (1765 – 1837), last of the Hanoverians, a dynasty notorious for its enormous sexual appetite and inclination towards scandal and insanity. But alas, her namesake daughter did not qualify as future Queen of England. Instead, her unremarkable and troublesome brother Bertie, only one year younger, would much later have to shoulder the heavy burden of the crown.

Sun/Jupiter trine Pluto in the 1st, ruler of the 8th in Aries, stands for a will of iron. But since Aries is intercepted and the chart ruler Neptune is in the 12th, all Plutonian ambitions are likely to get stuck and frustrated in a cul-de-sac. Another poignant placement is Mars, the co-ruler of the 1st and traditional ruler of Scorpio. Sitting on the descendant, the red planet is activated not only by partners but also by open enemies, of whom there will be quite a few during her life. And Mars is in the 7th, where we find also the Moon, ruler of the 5th, where Chiron is placed.

An alien at the Prussian court

Just as the 13-year-old Elizabeth Windsor would fall in love instantly with Prince Philip (of Greece and Denmark) ninety years later, so the tiny 15-year-old Vicky fell quickly for handsome and tall Fritz, heir to the Prussian throne. His ascendant is at 29° Scorpio, sitting right on her Sun/ Jupiter conjunction; the perfect mate to hero-worship. His Saturn sits on her challenged Virgo Mars on the descendant with its manifold aspects. He is a worthy replacement for her adored father: German, good natured and, most of all, someday King of Prussia. Nay, even Emperor of Germany, outranking Queen Victoria as head of European royals, who will soon enough become Empress of India in order not to be overshadowed; but all this lies in the future.

Her parents were delighted by the match. Now the torch of British liberalism could be handed over to the backward reactionary Prussia in order to strengthen the Anglo-German relationship and secure peace in Europe. How naïve! Vicky, although speaking perfect German (albeit with a slight accent) wasn't at all welcome in Potsdam. Her many accomplishments were seen as sheer arrogance; her political ambitions and interest in science and philosophy were frowned upon. Her bitterest enemy was Bismarck, the iron chancellor, who didn't trust the British and rather wanted to strengthen the ties between France and Russia.

Her self-confident and commanding attitude (Pluto in 1st, Sun/ Jupiter in 8th, Lilith on MC) didn't help, either. Women at the Potsdam court were expected to be uneducated and submissive. She was clearly a misfit.

Problems of motherhood

The square between Pluto in the 1st (willpower), ruler of the 8th (self-conquest) with Chiron in the 5th, signifies issues with a wounded child (Chiron in the 5th). But Chiron also receives a trine from Sun/Jupiter and a sextile from Mars. In Vicky's case, this conflict was dealt with by a constant rollercoaster of ambivalence, poisonous for any child and the root of narcissistic damage in Wilhelm: he felt that he was a constant reminder of his mother's own failed ambitions and intellectual disappointment. Many mothers dealing with handicapped children can over-compensate by showering their offspring with love. But Vicky took a different line. She subtly transferred her love to her other seven children, all of them were perfectly healthy. Sigmund Freud later analysed this relationship and came to the conclusion that rather than the Kaiser's handicap, it was his mother's ambivalence and rejection that had eventually crushed his self-confidence and led him to act out so excessively as an adult.

Entangled in her contradictory feelings of shame, guilt and hope, Vicky subtly withdrew her desperately needed motherly support.

Unrequited love

In Wilhelm's chart both luminaries are dramatically involved with the paradoxical agendas of Uranus against Pluto. Uranus/Pluto frictions deal with, on the one hand, the contradictory needs for intimate closeness on the one side versus on the other, freedom and distance. Not only does the Sun in Aquarius in the 8th square Pluto in the 11th, it is also challenged in an opposition to Saturn in Leo in the 2nd. This makes Pluto the focal point of a T-square. Even more challenging, the Moon in Scorpio in the 5th opposes Uranus in the 11th, the houses of self-expression and society.

The Aquarius Sun widely conjoining Chiron signifies a wounded self-image, which fits with his physical handicap and its psychological implications. His adored, albeit distant father Friedrich, dies of laryngeal

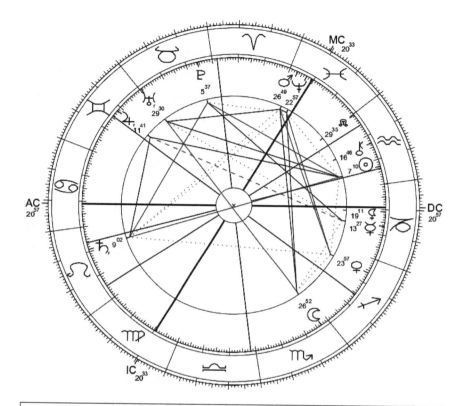

Emperor of Germany, Wilhelm II, 27 January 1859, 15:00 LMT, Potsdam, Germany, RR:B

8th house constellations

- Sun and Chiron in 8th
- Sun opposition Saturn in 2nd
- Sun square Pluto in 11th
- Sun trine Jupiter in 11th
- Sun rules 2nd and 3rd houses
- Uranus, ruler of 8th in 11th, opposition Moon in Scorpio

cancer. For this, Wilhelm knows who to blame: "An English doctor killed my father, and an English doctor crippled my arm – which is the fault of my mother". Wilhelm now succeeds to the throne, aged 29 years, exactly during his Saturn return. And in vengeance, he banishes his mother from court. She has to move to a castle near Frankfurt, which she buys from her own money, and where in her last years she will have to watch Wilhelm embark on a disastrous collision course with her own home country.

The feeling of powerlessness during his childhood was replaced starkly by his almost absolute power as monarch, so that he could over-compensate for his handicap. Given the German military state's extreme hierarchy and strict rules of obedience, it is not surprising that Wilhelm's Sun conjoins the MC of the German Reich (1871), a vivid analogue for over-compensation: the Kaiser as fatherly projection figure (Sun) representing (MC) the state.

In Wilhelm's chart, the ruler of the 11th house is Mars, conjunct Neptune in Pisces in the 10th house. When Mars and Neptune find themselves conjoined, they resort to all sorts of tricks to express themselves. Wilhelm camouflaged his handicap by learning to ride with one arm on a specially trained horse so that he could keep his balance or shoot with a special gun. When photographed, his left hand was either put nonchalantly in his jacket pocket or rested on a sabre. Over-compensation for his feeling of imperfection, he developed a fetish (Neptune) for uniforms and the military in general (Mars in the 10th, Neptune as ruler of MC in the 10th).

He hero-worships his father who fights in the decisive wars against Austria-Hungary and France, which will eventually trigger the formation of the German Reich in 1871. The crippled prince is surrounded by hyper-potent authority figures. Mars in Pisces conjunct Neptune on the MC is a powerful symbol for over-idolising the masculine leader archetype. This placement also fits perfectly with his early obsession with the navy. He is in total awe of the British fleet and the Empire.

Its embodiment, his almighty grandmother Victoria, is oddly enough, one of the few adults who can endear herself to the often erratic and bossy boy.

Love turns into hatred

Wilhelm, who longed for motherly attention and approval, must have felt the ambivalent feelings of his mother very severely. In later life he seems to have had the same ambivalence about any sort of relationship. To his six sons and one daughter he is a distant father and he is too busy travelling about to spend time with this wife.

During his time at boarding school, the teenage Wilhelm develops a sort of Oedipal crush on his mother. He continually sends her 'love letters' in which he confronts her with his longings. The objects, or rather the fetishes, of his dreams are her hands. In one letter he writes: "I have been dreaming about your dear soft, warm hands. I am awaiting with impatience the time when I can sit near you and kiss them but pray keep the promise you gave me, always to give me alone the soft inside of your hand to kiss, but of course you keep this a secret for yourself."

She feels overwhelmed and doesn't know how to respond. She sends his letters back, without referring to the content, but by correcting his grammar. This is the deathblow to his desires. From now on, he withdraws more and more, leaving her clueless as to why.

Contradictory agendas

In the composite chart of mother and son, the 8th house is unsurprisingly emphasised and connected by aspects and rulers with almost every other placement in the composite. The stellium in the 8th shows that both protagonists are entangled in a relationship of intense, contradictory feelings. Sun, Mercury and Venus might find each other's company quite agreeable, but it is Black Moon Lilith which is the odd one out in the group and very likely to act as troublemaker. In Capricorn, Lilith wants

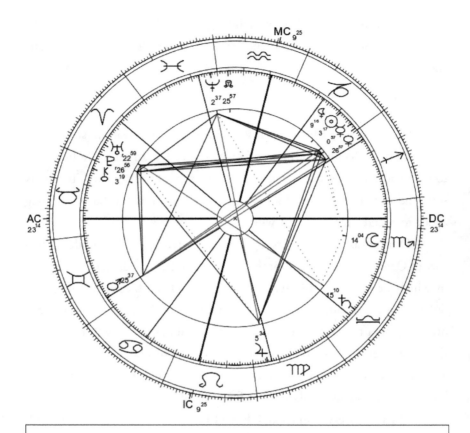

Empress Frederica/Emperor Wilhelm II - composite chart

8th house constellations

- Sun, Mercury, Venus and Lilith in 8th
- Sun trine Chiron in 12th
- Venus part of grand trine with Jupiter at cusp of 5th and Pluto in 12th
- Venus opposition Mars at cusp of 2nd
- Jupiter, ruler of 8th as base of a kite with opposition Neptune

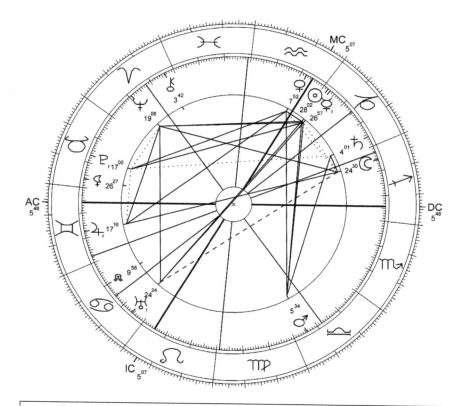

German Reich 18 January 1871, 12:40 LMT, Versailles, France

8th house constellations

- Saturn in Capricorn in 8th as ruler of 9th
- Saturn square Mars in Libra in 5th
- Saturn square Chiron in Aries in 11th
- Jupiter, ruler of 8th in 1st
- Jupiter opposition Moon in 7th
- Jupiter sextile Neptune in 12th

to challenge patriarchal rules within traditional hierarchies. Vicky is the daughter of the most influential woman of her time, so she knows about female power. Wilhelm adores his grandmother and later in life wants to overpower the British Empire by pushing the German Reich to the first row as a force to be reckoned with. In brief, Lilith stands for 'emancipation' which in this case is certainly most apt. While Vicky at least escapes her mother's court, Wilhelm seeks domination over the British Empire, represented by the female side of his ancestry.

The powerful kite figure with apex Neptune in the 10th on the cusp represents highly idealistic expectations, a search for vision which can (because Neptune is not the most realistic of planets) easily dissolve into illusion.

Jupiter at the base in opposition seems to say, "My battery is fully charged, let's kick off, I am hungry and adventurous". It also signifies high ambitions. The essential problem is that mother and son wanted something completely contradictory to their 10th house mission. Vicky, as product of her upbringing, had her parent's vision of a closely-knit liberal Anglo-European network, with her numerous siblings, nieces and nephews sitting on most of the thrones. Wilhelm, on the other hand, partly out of hatred and over-compensating competitiveness with the British Empire, wanted to isolate Germany from its neighbours and old allies.

Wilhelm's Sun conjoins the MC of the German Reich's MC; his ascendant conjoins its Uranus. Vicky's Chiron conjoins Germany's Uranus. The 8th house stellium in the composite stands in opposition to malefic Mars. As a boy he loved the idea of being half-British. Later he fell into a fatal collision with his mother's country and transferred his hatred of her to a loathing for Britain.

Of course, this is only one of many complex reasons which brought about WWI, but nevertheless a crucial one! One should not be tempted to take sides in this drama or oversimplify the principle of cause and effect. But one thing for me is quite clear: 8th house issues, if left unresolved, can develop an explosive momentum.

Princess Beatrice: At the mercy of a domestic tyrant

A pathological mother-daughter relationship

The deeply entangled and twisted relationship between Queen Victoria (1819 – 1901), and her youngest daughter, Princess Beatrice (1857 – 1944), is quite remarkable. As befits an 8th house story, it is both utterly sad and at the same time deeply touching. From the day her husband, Prince Albert, who dies at age 42, right until her own death, almost forty years later, Beatrice is held closely at her mother's side, as her aide and companion. At times, Beatrice is almost sucked dry by her domineering and demanding mother. At age 27, however, she flexes her muscles and insists to be allowed to marry and have a least some kind of independent life with a husband and children. After Victoria's death Beatrice destroys much of the queen's extensive correspondence and edits her diaries down to only one third of their original size. She does this, apparently by her mother's explicit wish, in order to prevent the revelation of anything which might cause insult or wreak any kind of havoc. Entanglement, border crossings, vampiric sucking out of someone else's energy, as well as hiding secrets are all 8th house issues. A veil of mystery lingers over this strange relationship. No wonder, given that both Victoria and Beatrice have Neptune in the 8th.

Neptunian symbiosis in the 8th

Neptune can cause a lot of chaos and confusion in the 8th house, especially when involved in a challenging aspect pattern. It can lure the native into becoming a victim of circumstances and other people's drama. One might feel forced to give all one's energy selflessly to others, but it can also work the other way around. In that case, the native with Neptune in the 8th might become particularly needy and demanding, not accepting other peoples' boundaries. Neptune often works in a strange sort of borderline mode. Pleasure and pain are subtly merged. Given that this planet rules idealistic and romantic hopes as well as harsh disappointments, its workings are seldom clear to the native.

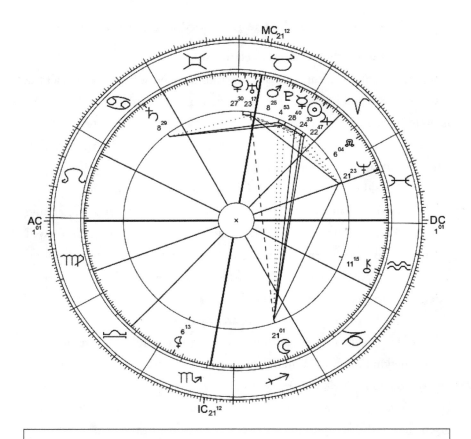

Princess Beatrice, 14 April 1857, 13:45 GMT, London, RR:A

8th house constellations

- Neptune in 8th as ruler of 8th
- Moon in 4th square Neptune
- Venus/Uranus in 10th sextile Neptune
- North Node in Aries in the 8th, square Saturn, quincunx Lilith

Important side note: Chiron in Aquarius in the 6th a singleton
in earth element

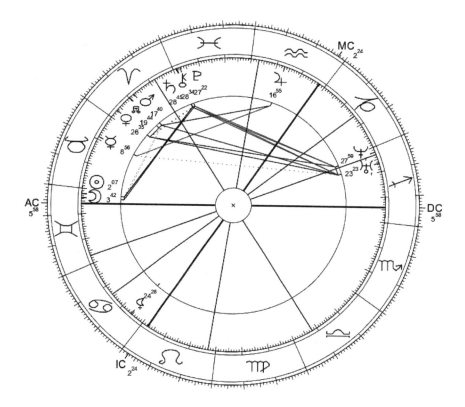

Queen Victoria, 24 May 1819, 04:15 LMT, London, RR:AA

8th house constellations

- Neptune in 8th as ruler of 11th (Pisces intercepted)
- Venus/Neptune trine
- Saturn/Chiron/Pluto in 11th square Neptune

Important side note: Mercury in Taurus in 12th as chart ruler is a singleton in earth element

Let's start with analysing Victoria's 8th house. Neptune in Sagittarius in the 8th rules, by way of interception, the 11th house of companionship and like-minded friends. It is also in a close square with a difficult triple conjunction between Saturn, Chiron and Pluto in Pisces in the 11th house. Saturn/Pluto in conjunction almost always hint at possessiveness and the extreme need for control and manipulation. Chiron, on the other hand, is the Achilles heel in the chart. This is where we feel most intimately hurt; a wound that can never quite fully heal. The mythological centaur Chiron figure is a sort of freak; half man, half horse. He has to hide from other people in order not to scare them. Blessed with incredible healing powers, he is – alas – not able to fully heal his own wounds.

Pairing harsh Saturn and Pluto with deeply vulnerable Chiron is complicated. Both Saturn and Pluto try their utmost to shield embarrassingly ugly Chiron from the outside world. Or, going to the other extreme, they become obsessed with the wound and try to force healing it in an extreme way. They may also manipulate everyone else into having a guilty conscience about this wound.

Claustrophobic conditions
As both a girl and adolescent, Victoria experiences a very isolated childhood. Her father, the Duke of Kent, dies when she is only six months old. She totally depends on her German mother Victoire of Saxe-Coburg-Saalfeld, who, without money or friends, finds herself totally out of depth in foreign London. Victoire's chart echoes Victoria's Saturn/Pluto conjunction in the 11th house. Also, her Moon sits directly at Victoria's Sun/Moon conjunction at the ascendent. Victoria's Neptune in the 8th forms a square with her mother's overcritical Mercury/Mars conjunction in Virgo. Victoire's Leo Sun forms a trine to her daughter's Neptune. The mother's main goal is to protect little Victoria, the heiress presumptive to the British throne. The girl is shielded from the court of her extravagant uncle, King William IV,

and is never allowed near other children. Victoria's closest companions were her huge collection of dolls, her dog and her devoted governess.

Her full 12th house with Mercury, Venus and Mars and Sun/Moon near the ascendant echoes the theme of being shut away. This theme is going to repeat itself later in life, albeit on a self-inflicted basis, when after Albert's death she becomes the reclusive 'widow of Windsor'.

The need for a father figure

While Victoria has to grow up without a father, this doesn't mean that there is no male influence at all. But it isn't a positive one. John Conroy, comptroller of her mother's household, holds a tight grip over the duchess and her daughter. His agenda is to have as much influence as possible over the future monarch in order to secure money and patronage for his career. History paints him as a rather evil and sinister character, with charisma and natural authority. The isolated widow totally depends on him in every matter of life. Anxious and overprotective herself, she wants to be as close to Victoria as possible. They even sleep in the same room, right until the day the girl becomes queen, at the age of 18.

The striking conjunction of Sun and Moon at the end of the 12th house, only a couple of degrees away from the ascendant, is a key placement in Victoria's chart. This pattern can often be found in charts of natives who have a very good idea of who they are. The conscious (Sun), as well as the unconscious (Moon) part of personality merge perfectly, thus supporting an authentic, unfeigned character. On an archetypical level, it is the pairing of the male (Sun) and the female (Moon), of father and mother, man and woman. Over her whole life, Victoria craves the support and adoration of strong men. The absence of a positive father figure leaves a deep hole in her complicated and often troubled psyche.

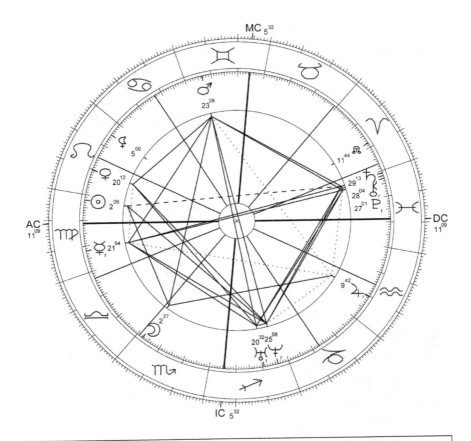

Prince Albert, 26 August 1819, 06:00 LMT Coburg, Germany, RR:B

8th house constellations

- North Node in Aries in 8th
- Mars, ruler of 8th, in Gemini in 10th as part of a grand cross
    square Mercury R in Virgo in 1st
    square Saturn/Chiron/Pluto in Pisces in 7th
    opposition Uranus/Neptune in Sagittarius in 4th
- Mars sextile Venus in Leo in 12th

In a conjunction, the Sun is not complete without the Moon and vice versa.
Take her extreme sympathy for some of her prime ministers. At the
beginning of her reign, she adores flirtatious Lord Melbourne. And later
in life her friendship with Benjamin Disraeli, whom she showers with
gifts, has no limits. She worships her husband, Prince Albert, almost like
a semi-god. And during her widowhood she transfers her need for a man
to her Scottish companion John Brown, and, during her last years, her
Indian attendant Abdul Karim. Both are very controversial figures and the
source of scandalous gossip. Consequently, Beatrice sees that much of her
mother's thoughts and feelings about these men are erased from her diaries.

Albert

Victoria falls passionately in love with Albert. The marriage, however,
causes problems on various levels. Her politicians, as well as the country at
large, are against the idea of importing an impoverished princeling from
an obscure German duchy. Also, Albert is not a sympathetic figure. He is
disliked for being a snobbish intellectual with no sense of humour and a
strong dislike for company and socialising. He is much better cut out for
the life of a reclusive professor. It is like planting someone in foreign soil.
Albert, although working obsessively for social and cultural innovations,
never quite warms to the British and vice versa. He is homesick for most of
the time, but much worse is the clash of characters between him and his
wife, for which there is striking proof in the synastry.

In Albert's chart the mutable cross is dominant; he has to adapt
flexibly to a multitude of external factors in the course of his short life. A
Sun in Virgo in the 12th house and Virgo rising with Moon in Scorpio,
he hides his emotions and is a sucker for hard work. Mercury retrograde
in the 1st is in opposition with Saturn/Pluto in the 7th. Mars in the 10th
is in opposition with Neptune/Uranus in the 4th house. These all come
together in a grand mutable cross, a recipe for burnout. Albert's Mars is
in opposition to Victoria's Neptune in the 8th. Her Venus opposes his

Jupiter. Her Moon in Gemini is inconjunct his Moon in Scorpio. They have rows all the time. He tries to tame her volcanic nature and teach her self-restraint, but in vain. He punishes her by withholding his love. She, in turn, is full of remorse and promises to better herself. At least from Victoria's side, there is a strong sexual attraction to Albert. Although most of her diary entries were later edited by Beatrice, some fragments survive where she finds herself in ecstasy watching him shave and dress and remarking that he didn't wear any undergarments under his tight pants.

Sex and pregnancy

Contrary to what we associate with Victoria, she absolutely loves sex. Needless to say, the inevitable side effect of sex in pre-contraception times is pregnancy. Unfortunately, Victoria hates being pregnant and has little affection for small children. In the period from 1840 to 1857, nine children arrive with monotonous regularity. Today we know a lot about postnatal depression, but in the 19th century women are just expected to pull themselves together and accept their fate in life. With every pregnancy she has to give more power over to Albert, the prince consort, who full-heartedly plunges himself in work. He takes an interest in almost every little detail of how the royal household, as well as the country, is run and wants to see modernisation everywhere. His most accomplished project is the Great Exhibition of 1851.

He also draws up exhausting education plans for all of his nine children and is really strict. Victoria's and Albert's masterplan is to mould a morally perfect royal dynasty and marry their children off over the whole of Europe and Russia. Vicky, the eldest, is almost a little mini Albert; super intelligent and mature. The heir, Bertie, however, is much less promising. He is slow and irritable. Victoria is overly possessive about Albert and jealous of her children. Neptune in the 8th comes more and more to the fore with advancing years. She becomes dependent on Albert and very demanding.

Having to share his affection with their nine children and his many other interests drives her nearly crazy at times.

1861: An annus horribilis

In early 1861, her mother dies of cancer. After the coronation Victoria shuns the duchess at court and maintains a very aloof and cold relationship with her. She simply wants to break with her lonely childhood and punishes both Conroy and her mother. But by now, over the months before her death Victoria begins to realise how cruel she has been to her mother and is full of remorse. When she finally dies, Victoria is shaken and heart-broken. She refuses to go out and only allows very few people around her: Albert, Beatrice and another of her daughters, Alice.

Fate strikes again, and this time much more severely. On 14 December, 1861, Albert dies of typhoid fever. Today, historians think that he had also been suffering from Crohn's disease, an inflammatory bowel condition. For Victoria, the loss of Albert, the companion on whom she had become so totally dependent, could not have been more catastrophic. He was her surrogate father figure, protector, guide and adviser in all and everything. To some extent he was even her mother, as well as her husband. The 42-year-old widow's grief is overbearing in the extreme and would come to dominate the royal household and the nation for decades.

Pathological grief disorder

Grief can become pathological when it persists and threatens to become chronic; Victoria refuses to carry out her day-to-day tasks. Losing Albert, the love of her life, amounts to traumatic stress injury.

In 1861, transiting Neptune sits at Victoria's Saturn/Chiron/Pluto conjunction and forms a square with her natal Neptune. Pluto conjoins natal Mercury in Taurus in the 12th house. Mercury in Taurus is a placement which often comes with a tendency to repeat familiar rituals again and again. Since Mercury is the chart ruler, this transit is of particular significance.

Pluto activates a mental mechanism of brooding and obsessive clinging to the past; a complete refusal to adapt to changes and let go of old business.

A vampiric relationship

Besides 4-year-old Beatrice, it falls on 18-year-old Alice to take on the burden of looking after Victoria. Alice had already been her father's nurse during his last and fatal illness. Now, instead of being allowed to mourn the loss of her beloved father, she, in a sense, almost has to take his place. Alice, with a full 12th house and Moon and Venus in Pisces, comforts her mother and is a rock of stability. That is, at least she pretends to be, as she is not allowed to cry in front of the queen. But alone in her room, she lets out her own grief. Over the following months she acts as her mother's secretary and intermediary with the government. She practically has to shoulder the bulk of the monarch's official business. The results of all this work are severe. The pretty young woman turns into an anorexic wreck. Her German fiancé hardly recognises her when he comes to visit. It's a horrible sensation for Victoria, to have to let go of Alice, but go she must, given that the match was Albert's own doing. Alice marries, Victoria has to consent.

Now the burden falls on Beatrice. In 1861 and 1862, Neptune is in opposition to Beatrice's Saturn. This kicks off a pattern which will come to full fruition over the next two decades. Saturn/Neptune combinations often deal with depression and melancholy. Beatrice has to comfort (Neptune) her mother and become her rock (Saturn). By doing this, she suppresses (Saturn), her own grief about the loss (Neptune) of her father. Another significant transit at this time is Lilith opposite natal Pluto. Lilith deals with emancipation and now experiences a first taste of powerlessness (Pluto).

Now she becomes her mother's main focal point and cannot leave her side. Her sisters Helena and Louise are dealing with Victoria's correspondence while she is still too young for this. Her main job is that of grievance toy and constant companion. She has to play the piano, read and keep the domineering matriarch entertained. That said, the royal household is in strict mourning. Light colours, joy and laughter are strictly prohibited. The children are sent to bed early and have to tiptoe around the house. And while not up to entertaining guests, Victoria still demands to be informed about everything concerning the remaining children.

This is a perverse repetition of Victoria's own forced symbiotic maternal relationship. Beatrice is now in danger of becoming babyfied for the rest of her life, but instead of staying a child, something quite contradictory happens. Beatrice appears to take on a number of the characteristics of a much older person. For instance, she begins to suffer rather severely from rheumatism. Her figure fills out, she becomes quite portly. This is a typical 8th house mechanism: the vampiric feeding off the energy of another being. Victoria has already lost her eldest daughter Vicky to Germany and now Alice. She is jolly well determined to keep her other three daughters close by, but beautiful Louise is a troublemaker and Helena is boring. Both will finally break free as well. Helena, however, is only allowed to marry an impoverished princeling and forced to live with her husband in Windsor castle. Selfish Victoria fights hardest to keep Beatrice by her side and does her utmost to put her daughter off marriage. Dinner guests are reprimanded by Victoria for mentioning the words engagement or wedding in the princess's presence.

Moon, Venus and Lilith under scrutiny

In Beatrice's chart the dominant elements are earth and fire. These contradictory elements are not easy to combine. While fire wants immediate action and follows its impulses, earth is much more cautious and needs security. In most cases, the native only fully owns either one or the other at a time. When occasion calls, the other dominant element can come to the fore, pushing the other to the background again. But on the whole, one element often feels more familiar, thus taking precedence over the other. In order to work together, fire has to let go of many ambitious plans, because earth would consider them as not being worth the trouble to get involved. Earth would pick up only a few of the many projects, weigh the options and move slowly and methodically into action.

With both luminaries in fire, and a packed 9th house, there is certainly a fair amount of curiosity and idealism going on. But let's not jump to hasty conclusions. Mars, ruler of Aries, is in Taurus, the sign of its fall, and conjunct Pluto. This is a sign of deep inner, suppressed passion mixed with a tendency to be defensive. Mars/Pluto only comes out fighting when pushed to the extreme. Or, as is often the case with Mars in Taurus, when something exceptionally desirable is in sight. The chart also displays a lack of air. The only placement in this element is the singleton Chiron in Aquarius in the 6th house of serving and health.

In love: Beatrice flexes her muscles
In 1884, despite the monarch's scheming, Beatrice, the most obedient of Victoria's five daughters, makes a bid for freedom. Aged 27, she falls in love with Henry, Prince of Battenberg and announces she wants to marry. This is the great moment of baby Beatrice flexing her muscles; the only really independent action of her life.

1885 is the year in which Mars goes over Beatrice's ascendent. Jupiter supports this infusion of energy by forming trines to all her Aries planets. The 1884/1885 solar return has Jupiter at the descendant, which is always a good indicator for an important encounter with a potential partner. We also have Sun square Jupiter and Black Moon Lilith, which stands for emancipation, trine Jupiter. Jupiter has a longing to spread out, especially when in a square. The Sun also is in a quincunx with Uranus, which vividly illustrates the difficult situation. Sun in the 2nd wants to focus on security, Uranus in the 8th longs for transformation and intimate encounters. Since the 8th house is also the house of sexuality and it is safe to assume that Beatrice is, at age 27, still a virgin, Uranus really wants to break free by seeking sensual intimacy. She is so in love that she puts her foot down, rather uncharacteristically. The dramatic frictions can be traced by the Sagittarius Moon on the MC, in opposition to Venus/Saturn and Chiron/Pluto.

Both the Moon and MC can be associated with the mother figure. And the opposing four planets, all assembled around the IC and the 4th house, keep on nagging for a change at home. Interestingly, this stellium almost identically repeats Victoria's triple conjunction of Saturn, Chiron and Pluto. And just as Victoria was helpless against her mother and John Conroy as a girl, she now wants to limit Beatrice's movement.

The Queen is not amused

Victoria throws one of her famous temper tantrums. It is an unspeakable outrage. Her response to Beatrice's wish to marry is probably one of the cruellest things that she does in her whole life. For about six months Victoria simply stops talking to her altogether. She communicates with her daughter only with little notes. Sitting at lunch together, she would pass her a note, while her eyes are averted. How does a daughter dare to go against her mother's and the monarch's will? Eventually, Victoria gives in to tenacious Beatrice. The wedding is allowed to go ahead, but only under the condition that the married couple will always remain with the Queen at Windsor. That way she can keep her companion and secretary close at hand. Apparently, Henry doesn't object, given that he is rather short of money. They have four children and Beatrice has found a compromise. Sadly, Henry dies from malaria during a trip abroad, aged only 37. This is another parallel between mother and daughter; the early loss of a husband.

Mother-daughter synastry

Both women have Neptune in the 8th house. Uranus, as modern ruler of Aquarius, can also be termed a planet of friendship and companionship, albeit not always in a conventional way. Victoria's Uranus/Neptune conjunction sits right on Beatrice's Moon, thus activating their Moon/ Neptune square.

Legacy whitewashing

The Queen dies in 1901. Jupiter forms a trine with Beatrice's ascendant, while Neptune forms a sextile to her natal Sun. Neptune is retrograde and will influence her Sun for quite a while. Since this is a constructive aspect, Neptune brings the native to a place of peace and forgiveness. And while Neptune is also a creative force, it also rules Beatrice, who has been acting as the Queen's secretary and aide for such a long time, now decides to commence a mammoth task: to whitewash her mother's legacy. This is by no means extraordinary for that time. The descendants of Jane Austen, for example, had edited and destroyed a bulk of her correspondence and diaries, in order to present a proper and morally intact image to the public. As a result, the collective unconsciousness still thinks of Austen as a prudish and rather dull matron. In recent years, however, other sources reveal that she had a very different personality and was sharp and witty; not at all easy to shock and a very observant psychologist in her own way.

With Victoria, and all her 12th house planets, we must ask ourselves the following question: did she ever contemplate publishing her innermost thoughts and gossip? Probably not. She had never been one to hold back her opinions and was not at all discreet. Intimate details about the relationships with the rough John Brown, who bullied her children and her household, and who had a strong influence on her, and the Indian servant, Abdul Karim, who became her close confidant, were highly scandalous and potential sources of embarrassment for the royal family. The only letters of Victoria's that survive are those she sent to her many acquaintances and mostly to her eldest daughter, Vicky. The bulk of her own, private thoughts were edited by Beatrice. In many ways, she, the babyfied, loyal daughter, had the final say in the story.

6
Resilience and Transformation

Yes, your transformation will be hard. Yes, you will feel frightened, messed up and knocked down. Yes, you'll want to stop. Yes, it's the best work you'll ever do.
Robin Sharma

Nothing happens until the pain of remaining the same outweighs the pain of change.
Arthur Burt

Pandora's Box holds hope at the very bottom, underneath all the pain and drama, so it is worth digging into the shadows of our 8th house. Transformation can only happen if there is a considerable shift in an individual's thought and behaviour patterns, which requires a major change in thought patterns and values.

Life can be a rollercoaster and often our unresolved issues from the past come back to haunt us. In my work as a psychotherapist I am often confronted with my clients' fear of change, another, less elaborate word for transformation. Clients are often unhappy with their present lives, sometimes traumatised by their past and very often daunted by the future. To free ourselves from unhealthy patterns, we have to try out other, more constructive patterns. On the other hand most of us prefer to stay in an unpleasant and frustrating status quo rather than try out something new. Well, I say: blame it all on good old ambivalence.

Ambivalence is a state of having simultaneous conflicting reactions, beliefs, or feelings towards some object. ...

> Explicit ambivalence may or may not be experienced as psychologically unpleasant when the positive and negative aspects of a subject are both present in a person's mind at the same time.
>
> *Wikipedia*

Life is full of possibilities and choices. Or is it? Do we just react to what life throws at us? Or are we genuinely free to create the life that we want for ourselves? The reality is often in-between, in my experience. We don't want to regret a decision afterwards and suffer the disappointment of having made a mistake. Often the decision *for* something means a decision *against* something. This can be daunting. After all, you can't have your cake and eat it. And yet, nothing is more painful than having to regret what we didn't do. Avoiding change can become pathological and lead to depression, bitterness and fear.

During my research for this book I came across the term resilience, and was intrigued. Basically, it means the psychological ability to cope with a crisis and survive unscathed, or rather – like a phoenix from the ashes – rise again with new powers. Know thyself...

I chose Dame Jane Goodall and RuPaul Charles as protagonists for this chapter because they represent courage and fearlessness. Dame Jane suffered horribly when she had to witness how her gentle chimps turned into killers. A typical 8th house phenomenon. There is a dark side to every creature. Also, to further her career as a primatologist in Africa, she had to part with her son Grub and send him to live with her mum in the UK. This almost broke her heart, but the two of them have stayed close ever since, somehow making their bond even stronger.

I adore RuPaul. I watch seasons of *Drag Race* again and again, some episodes I have probably watched a dozen times. Not only am I entertained by the glamour and talent, but also by the many touching personal stories of the contestants who were often bullied and humiliated for being gay and behaving out of the gender-box. By creating this huge platform, RuPaul enables countless people who feel like outsiders in society to find a community where they can connect and find encouragement.

Lilith, Drag Queens and Breaking Gender Stereotypes

The Black Moon Lilith point can denote the search for one's own sexuality and gender role and a rejection of the patriarchal order, as is evident in the charts of RuPaul and his hit TV show. Both charts also show that the 8th house plays an important role. After all, transformation and resilience are key factors both for drag as well as for the 8th house.

Lilith: myth and adaptability

Black Moon Lilith (BML) is the hot topic *du jour* in astrology. Many astrologers are exploring this fascinating topic, trying to make sense of Lilith, the dark side of the moon, which is a point, not a planet. In my chart I have her directly on my MC, so she must be of some significance to me, I reckon. The problem is, I don't know in what way. I have read over a dozen books about Lilith. Unfortunately, I still haven't quite got my head around her. It's frustrating and I don't think it does her justice to boil her essence down merely to 'emancipation'. Since it involves values, sexuality, shadow work and transformation, I feel that it has some relevance for the 8th house.

For this reason, I conducted my own research in order to make the ancient Lilith myths usable for modern chart interpretation.

Her mythical provenance is easy to relate, though there are different versions. The beginning is easy enough. Lilith was the first wife of Adam, before the much more famous and familiar Eve. The two women were very different, almost like the proverbial good and bad sisters in a fairytale. But Lilith was there first, and, unlike Eve, was not created from one of Adam's ribs. Instead, just like Adam, she was born of the dust of the earth, and as his companion in Eden she was his equal. Well, not quite. When it came to sexual intercourse, she was not supposed to be on top; she had to content herself with the rule-book missionary position. This restriction made her furious. She just wouldn't budge and rebelled by taking God's name in vain. In consequence, she either vanished voluntarily or was banished from paradise by Him. Adam, on the other hand, wanted her back, interestingly. Lilith took to living in the wilderness and consorting with demons, brooding on revenge. Some sources claim that she disguised herself as the infamous snake and seduced Eve to eat the apple. Other stories say she was divinely punished with barrenness or sexual partners made sterile. She craved motherhood and stole babies from other women, making her a very scary archetype, both to men and women.

It strikes me that this figure is so negative and unsympathetic. How am I supposed to work with this point in a chart? Aren't there pieces missing in this puzzle? Was Adam really averse to a little experimental spice in his sex life? Why did he miss Lilith? And what about Eve? Were they rivals or friends? Or a little bit of both? This is important when touching on issues such as feminist solidarity and abuse, e.g. the #MeToo movement. And why was Lilith denied children?

While the Moon represents what is most familiar to us, Black Moon Lilith is what is hidden from view, blocked from sight and thus difficult to feel consciously. It is obvious that this fierce and powerful female archetype is at odds with tradition and patriarchal-dominated gender stereotypes. It goes against everything 'normal' in society and is contra the God-given order. Lilith says 'No' to what is expected of her (by a male God) and wants to find her own way of expressing her femininity. Since this may be particularly frightening to men of traditional cultural expression and thinking, the witch archetype must be punished.

The Moon has to do with biological fecundity, Lilith has to do with fecundity on other levels.
Lynn Bell

Lilith deals with finding one's own sexuality and gender role by saying 'No' to the patriarchal order, finding one's own fecundity and seeking equal status. In a female chart, it can be enlightening to explore what Lilith wants to say. But what about the Black Moon in a male chart?

Is there a male equivalent to misogyny?

The answer is: yes. It is called 'misandry' – a hatred of men. Here I must tell you of a personal encounter I had last year. I am still unsure whether I was exposed to a case of misandry or not. It was shortly before I was due to fly to Vienna to give a talk about Lilith and repressed femininity in male charts. I had dinner with a couple of astrology-savvy mates and wanted to share an example of how Black Moon Lilith could be expressed in a man's chart. In recent years, in trendy areas of Berlin, I have noticed that more and more fathers are proudly out and about with their infants. They seem to embrace a new, modern kind of fatherhood; more caring, gentle and affectionate, for the whole world to see. They strut around with their babies symbiotically attached to their chest. A sign of liberation from ancient role stereotypes of one-dimensional rough-and-tumble macho men who are not allowed to show their more tender emotions in public. To care for a child is traditionally a lunar activity, thus a female and maternal issue and not typically a male one. I, for one, am always rather touched when I see these 'new men' and find it utterly endearing.

However, this was obviously not the case with the woman who sat next to me. She looked irritated and burst out: "But wouldn't this overly motherly behaviour castrate a man's Mars?" Interesting, I thought. Why was she so contemptuous? Is this a typical reaction? Is she projecting her own unembraced Lilith side onto these men? I had a sudden flashback to my own childhood. It reminded me of a story my dad had once told me. When his mates found out that he changed nappies, he became the butt of all kinds of jokes, some of them even questioning his masculinity.

Surely we are experiencing the dawning of a New Age of sensitive, caring manhood. Well, not entirely, because every trend creates a contra-trend. Here, Jacob Rees-Mogg (Leader of the House of Commons at the time of writing) springs to mind, a father of six, who prides himself on never having changed a nappy in his life; he just wasn't 'modern enough'. He also vehemently condemns abortion as a sin and opposes gay marriage. In his chart, Lilith is in maternal Cancer, in a square to Chiron in Aries. Does the chart show us some repressed maternal issues here? What strikes me as remarkable is that he showed up at an official function with his old nanny and looked untypically mellow and tame. Lilith is a feminine archetype, together with Moon and Venus. Men can transfer these energies to the women in their life or try to own them, sometimes both. Rees-Mogg clearly rather projects Lilith instead of owning her. 'Lilith issues' often manifest as repressed and rejected facets of femininity. These facets might remain unconscious and repressed because of the shame and helplessness that they involve. It is obvious that it can affect women, but what about men?

On the same day, I came across a picture of veteran Hollywood actor Donald Sutherland with his 40-year-old son Kiefer sitting on his dad's lap at a gala. How fun is that? Donald has a Venus/Neptune/Lilith/conjunction in the 12th house in a trine with Uranus in the 8th. Apparently these men do not have a problem with showing softer emotions in public. Disarming, I thought.

RuPaul - Doing drag can be a way of making peace with a dark childhood

Drag queen superstar RuPaul Charles is a genuine force of nature, but not easy to pin down genderwise. You can call RuPaul she or he, it's not important, Ru owns both genders. With an estimated net worth fortune of $60 million to his name, this successful musician, TV host, entertainer and activist for LGBTQ rights is a Jack and Jane of all trades. RuPaul always makes a huge and impressive impact, helped by his/her skyscraper height of 6ft 4ins, rising to 7ft in high heels. You can't overlook Ru! Be it as the eleganty lanky bold man in slick designer suits, or as the blond drag queen with her iconic padded hour glass figure and ferocious temperament, to me, RuPaul perfectly embodies a 21st century Lilith archetype. At the same time he is a good example of how to deal with Plutonic and 8th house issues. From early childhood he lived with strong women – his mother, grandmother and sisters, while his father was absent. Ru always felt like an alien (Sun in Scorpio square Uranus) and was always being picked on by his peers, feeling left out and rejected. At the same time he longed to perform, show off and entertain people. His packed 5th house, with a powerful trio of Moon, Mercury and Neptune in Scorpio, longs to play around, become different characters and seek confrontation. Lilith in the 2nd (talents and self-esteem) forms a supportive trine, as if she wants to give her blessing. On the other hand, Lilith forms a conjunction with Mars and a wide opposition to Saturn, ruler of the 8th. This means that issues of self-confrontation and transformation seem unavoidable.

During his Saturn return he decided to pull himself together and overcome his inner saboteur. The feeling of rejection was almost insufferable at this time. While he feels rejected by white people because he was black, black people reject him for being gay. Gay people on the other hand often look down on him because he is too effeminate. So, at age 28, Ru decides that he is not going to have it anymore. Another strong woman, Oprah

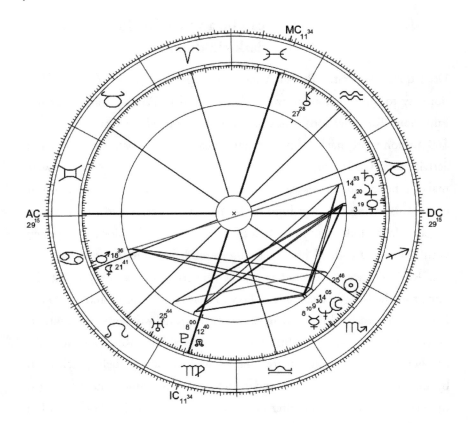

RuPaul Charles, 17 November 1960 18:52 PST, San Diego, California, RR:AA

8th house constellations

- Saturn as ruler of 8th in 7th
- Mars/Lilith opposition Saturn
- Saturn trine Pluto/IC
- Saturn sextile Moon/Mercury/Neptune

Winfrey (who has Lilith at the MC), saves Ru because he loves watching her shows and feels empowered by her.

What follows is a career in the club scene of New York, doing gigs and hosting radio and TV shows, both in and out of drag. When Ru talks about *Drag Race*, the Scorpio/8th house side shines through. The challenges are compared with the process of dying and being reborn. He challenges the contestants to go beyond their own limited perception of themselves.

The Drag Queen: A modern Lilith archetype

The drive to create a strong female character can be seen as a subconscious desire to protect oneself against a world of discrimination - as in the case of RuPaul and countless other drag queens. Drag queens are super-feminine heroines, an over-exaggerated version of what a woman might be like when she is almighty and placed on a pedestal, almost like a goddess. If we look back at how Lilith in the myth gets humiliated because she wants to lie on top of Adam, (not be passively stuck under him) we understand it is about sexual desire and role-play. Today, sexuality isn't necessarily linked with traditional gender roles.

We're all born naked and the rest is drag (RuPaul)

In the chart of RuPaul Charles, Saturn is the ruler of the 8th house and interwoven in powerful aspect patterns, reflecting his lifelong struggle to overcome his shyness. He often speaks about overcoming his inner saboteur, which can be categorised as an 8th house mechanism. By creating a drag persona he transforms into someone who is brave, courageous and daring. At the same time, he feels more empowered as an out-of-drag man to be a fighter for LGBTQ-rights.

Drag doesn't change who you are, it actually reveals who you are. RuPaul

RuPaul's Drag Race was first aired in 2009, in a niche gay format. It took a couple of years until it hit the zeitgeist and it has since become phenomenally

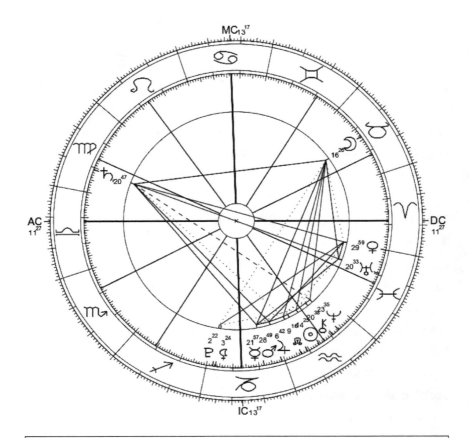

RuPaul's *Drag Race*, 2 February 2009, 22:00 EST, New York

8th house constellations

- Moon in Taurus in 8th
- Moon is part of a grand trine with Saturn in 12th and Mercury in 4th
- Moon squares Sun/Chiron in Aquarius in 5th
- Moon sextile Uranus in 6th
- Moon rules the MC

popular, even winning an Emmy. Surprisingly, there is no fire at all in this chart, except for South Node in Leo. Isn't that odd? After all, the reality competition show is all fireworks and as fierce as a flame-thrower. The winner receives a cash prize of $100,000 and all the recognition that comes with the winner's title, 'America's Next Drag Superstar'.

The queens not only have to fight for their glamorous moments in the spotlight, they must compete in sawing, singing, dancing, acting and 'reading and roasting'. Above all, they have to hit the runway ("Now, sissy that walk") in death defying high heels, obnoxiously padded hourglass figures and Oscar night make-up. But none of this is enough. Contestants must also use their sharp elbows, long acrylic claws and acid tongues to impress the judges. Each episode culminates in an outrageous 'lip synch for your life' showdown in which the two weakest queens mime and strut to a pop diva's hit song in a battle to stay in the show, like a gladiatorial display in the Roman Coliseum. This often ends up in tears. The loser is sent home to RuPaul's brutal words "Sashay away", while the victor is told "Shantay, you stay". Sometimes the two contestants will have bonded during the preceding stressful weeks, but more often than not the winner is glad to see the rival go. "I'll help her packing, that stupid, shady ho."

In a personal chart the absence of fire can indicate a lack of drive and trust in one's mojo. You might also find it in the chart of late bloomers. To compensate for this elemental lack, one has to connect with deep inner passions (water), focus on a concrete goal (earth), and meet career opportunities with curiosity and flexibility (air).

It is a rather baffling paradox that an absence of fire can make a person come across as super-fiery. Libra rising (in the show's chart) indicates the importance of fair play and a polished appearance. Beauty is key in *RuPaul's Drag Race*. Venus is in mysterious and oscillating Pisces in the industrious 6th house. So in this show Venus may be invited to a fancy-dress party, but she has to do all the work. The queens themselves design, sew and hot-glue together their unique costumes as well as paint their faces to look like goddesses. It's hard labour, quite like in a Dickensian sweat shop. The final drag 'look' may resemble Cruella de Ville, Diana Ross or Lady Gaga. Frogs turned into princesses. Very Cinderella!

The ever-present moaning mantra of the contestants is: "Bitch, the struggle is getting real!" Moon in Taurus in the 8th forms squares with the stellium in Aquarius in the 4th and 5th houses. Venus as ruler of the 8th finds herself tied up in a square with Lilith and Pluto in Capricorn in the 3rd. This clearly indicates the battle between the more playful, inventive and creative (Pisces) facets of femininity (Venus) and a fiercer, more angry side, which is a force to be reckoned with (Pluto/Lilith). A regular bitch fest! And then take a look at who Venus has as roommate in the 6th: there's Uranus also, master of the unexpected and shocking - guru of aliens, misfits and 'pink sheep'. The planet of freedom is at the apex of a kite which takes off from retrograde Saturn in Virgo in the 12th house. This is a very delicate placement, never mind the fact that it is in the place of Joy in Hellenistic astrology. Psychologically it often indicates a fear of being alone, an inability to relax and let go.

This is a powerful motivation for a kite! Overcome the restrictions of Saturn (RuPaul's cheer: "Good luck, and don't fuck it up") and strive for freeing yourself through hard work (6th house). This is very apt for a show which has won many awards and has empowered not only the LGBTQ movement, but has also contributed to freeing many women to play around with the different facets of their femininity. They can be coy, seductive, aggressive, obnoxious, alluring, funny and yet authentic. It is not necessarily about making yourself attractive to others, but rather to celebrate your own glamorous self. When I went to a RuPaul show in Hamburg, I was amazed that the majority of the audience were female. Many female fans of the show admire the drag queens' courage and guts. They can identify with their struggles and victories and see proof that whatever your size, colour, age or background, you can free yourself from restrictive role model requirements, mostly dictated by (straight) men.

The striking stellium in eccentric Aquarius includes the Sun conjoined with wounded Chiron and oscillating Neptune as the third, and ambitious Jupiter as the fourth man on board. The North Node adds further momentum to the group, which is led by dreamy Neptune in the 5th house of showing off, spreading back to the 4th house of roots and deeper inner identity issues. Sun/Chiron can be nailed down to the fact that most of the contestants share a painful history of struggling as outsiders in a homophobic environment, often worsened by race issues. A wounded (Chiron) self (Sun), which tries, by acting (Neptune), to stay optimistic (Jupiter) on the karmic journey (North Node). As RuPaul always points out: "You have to show us your charisma, uniqueness, nerve and talent." Some moments are truly heart-breaking. Cameras are always at the ready; the show also documents the excessive preparation sessions in the work room when the fans get to witness their unbelievable transformations. It is often during these sessions that a queen feels like opening up to the other 'girls' to share her sad story of neglect, hardship, fear and humiliation. RuPaul always ends an episode with an almost religious mantra:

> "If you can't love yourself, how in the hell are you gonna love somebody else. Now can I get an Amen up in here?"

Jane Goodall: Pushing boundaries

I do have hope

It is easy to be overwhelmed by feelings of hopelessness as we look around the world. We are losing species at a terrible rate, the balance of nature is disturbed, and we are destroying our beautiful planet... But in spite of all this I do have hope.
Dame Jane Goodall

June 2020. Dame Jane Goodall, the famous primatologist and naturalist, raises a warning voice in the midst of the Covid-19 pandemic. At age 86, this courageous lady is more highly regarded all over the world than ever before, and serves as a role model for the many young people who admire her passion and devotion to her cause. She fears that humanity will soon be finished if we don't stop over-exploiting the natural world, with forests cut down, species made extinct and natural habitats destroyed. With her Sun in Aries conjunct Mars in the 4th house of roots, home and family, she is an astonishing example of what a single individual can achieve. Taking into account that she, as a woman in the 1950s, had a solid wall of misogyny against her, it is even more astonishing. But she persevered and still stands her ground, fearless and against all odds. Sun and Mars stand in opposition to Jupiter in the 10th and in square with Pluto/Lilith in the 8th, aligning to a powerful T-square. The Moon, as the ruler of the 8th, sits right on her optimistic Sagittarius ascendant, which accounts for her extraordinarily dignified and non-invasive charismatic aura.

Jubilee

Usually dads present their children with the obligatory teddy bear. Not so in Jane Goodall's case. Her father, the dashing racing car driver Mortimer Herbert Morris-Goodall, gives her a stuffed chimpanzee for her first birthday, whom she names Jubilee. This little stuffed creature ignites her lifelong passion for that particular species of chimpanzees. Even today, she still keeps Jubilee on her dresser in her flat in London.

Her general love for animals defines her whole childhood. She can watch the hens for hours and loves to look after the neighbourhood dog, Rusty. Other key sources of inspiration are Doctor Doolittle, who can communicate with animals and Tarzan, the famous jungle man. In the 1930s exciting female role models are scarce, so she decides to look at male heroes instead. Her mother supports her in this, agreeing that girls should not feel discouraged by the limited career choices for women. Jane simply longs for adventure. This yearning is so powerful that at night she often dreams that she is a man, typically a fearless adventurer.

A lack in earth

Her chart is lacking in earth, with Neptune in Virgo as a singleton. A lack in a certain element can make this element a focus point in life and signifier for an area of over-compensation. Earth is the element of nature, sensuality and responsibility. Neptune, on the other hand, is the planet of fantasy, altruism and love for other creatures. In the 9th, it activates everything exotic, deals with travelling and believes anything is possible. The sky is the limit. If we look for animals in the chart, they can be found in both the 9th house (big animals) and in the 6th house (pets). Jane has Chiron in the 6th house. If we look at her passion for nature and animals from childhood on, these placements make perfect sense. Taking also into account that Neptune, the planet of merging and idolizing, forms a wide square with Chiron in the 6th, we can guess how the story will go on. Chiron is a vital source in Jane's chart. It not only squares with Neptune, but also with her Venus/Saturn conjunction in Aquarius in the 3rd. Furthermore, it is in opposition with her Sagittarius Moon, which explains to a certain degree why she can sympathise so deeply with how vulnerable nature and animals are.

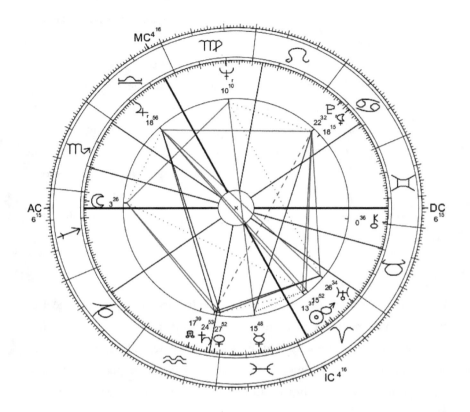

Jane Goodall, 3 April 1934, 23:30 GMT, Hampstead, England, RR:B

8th house constellations

- Pluto-Lilith in 8th
- Pluto ruler of 11th and 12th
- Moon, ruler of 8th, at ascendant
- Pluto apex of T-square with Uranus in 4th and Jupiter in 10th
- Pluto trine Mercury Pisces in 3rd
- Pluto quincunx Venus/Saturn in 3rd

The year that changes everything

Her beginnings are humble. Her family can't afford to send her to university, so she pragmatically acquires a secretarial certification and takes up a job as a waitress, to save money for a trip to Africa. This is her dream; she just has to get there, come what may. Then, in 1957, totally out of the blue, something wonderful happens. A friend in Kenya invites her for a visit. There she meets the famous palaeontologist Louis Seymour Bazett Leakey. The two hit it off instantly and she becomes his secretary. And, as another stroke of luck, it is around that time that Leakey applies for a grant to embark on a 6-month study of chimpanzees in their natural habitat. He seeks to gather important insight about early hominids' behaviour and evolution. For this job he would favour someone who is preferably unbiased by scientific theories. Jane has impressed him with her true passion for animals; she seems the perfect choice. Leakey, with Sun in Leo, has Jupiter in a trine with Jane's Pluto and vice versa; the perfect combination of adventurous and visionary (Jupiter) in-depth-research and border-crossings (Pluto).

The strange white ape

It is the 1950s, so one can hardly stress enough how totally revolutionary it is for a young woman to be alone in the African wilderness, only accompanied by a handful of helpers. Jane enjoys every minute of it. She feels that her childhood dreams have come true; she has become her own female version of Doctor Doolittle and Tarzan, all wrapped up together. Pluto in the 8th loves to cross boundaries and to break taboos. This placement also fits very well with research of all sorts and the unveiling of secrets, in order to come up with transformative, hitherto unknown insights.

Her Aries planets, on the other hand, simply live for the idea of being first, and marvel at the excitement. At first the task at hand seems almost impossible to tackle. Although she finds a chimpanzee community and follows them around, she can never get near. As soon as they get sight of her they run off, because they are suspicious of this strange white ape.

But Jane is persistent; there is just too much at stake, and she doesn't want to disappoint Leakey. Her tenacity pays off. Eventually, after a couple of months, the chimps get used to the strange white ape and allow Jane to get closer. Now, at last, she can finally observe them in close-up. The experience is totally mesmerising. She feels like a part of this magic animal world, which probably no other human has had the opportunity to witness before. Soon she finds out that the chimps form close social relationships, and show behaviour which is quite similar to that of humans. They interact in a caring, sensitive way and seek reassurance. She is intrigued, because this is a new way of approaching apes. Pluto in the 8th is truly in its element.

An amazing discovery

One day she watches some chimps on a termite mount. They pick up small leafy twigs, strip them of their leaves and then stick the twigs into a hole to retrieve some termites, which stick on the twig, so they can be eaten as a delicacy. It had long been thought that humans are the only species on earth that can make and use tools. But now, Jane's pioneering discovery simply must challenge this hypothesis. However, her findings do not go down well within the male-dominated scientific community. As a result, she finds herself discredited because of her gender, youth and the fact that she is untrained. Pluto in the 8th forms a conjunction with Lilith, so we are dealing here with rejected facets of the female archetype; a woman who dares to challenge the patriarchal order.

Lilith issues

In her 1957 solar return for Gombe, Pluto is in the 1st house, in opposition to Lilith and square the Moon in the 10th in Taurus, which is in a trine with Jupiter in Virgo in the 2nd. The Moon in Taurus and Jupiter in Virgo add some earth energy to her natal chart in this year, which will be so decisive for her. Pluto in the 1st stands for fearlessness and determination,

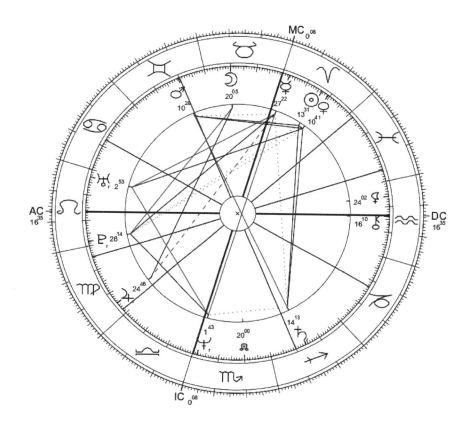

Jane Goodall solar return 1957

as well as a willingness to allow transformation. A year with the solar Moon in the 10th is often a time during which the native emotionally strongly identifies with career matters. Jupiter in critical and detail-oriented Virgo in the 2nd house activates Jane's talents, which might have been hidden before. Sun, Mercury and Venus stand in the 9th house of foreign affairs, travel and beliefs. The three form a wide grand trine with Saturn in the 5th and Uranus in the 12th, thus bringing both discipline and independence. Solar return Lilith conjoins her natal Venus/Saturn conjunction, which is a vivid image for female empowerment (Lilith) via hard work (Saturn), in order to gain self-worth and pleasure (Venus). Furthermore, the Mercury/

Neptune opposition in the solar chart activates the natal Jupiter/Uranus opposition. To top it all off, solar return Chiron sits on the natal North Node, signifying that her calling (North Node), which has to do with healing (Chiron), is now activated and can come into full fruition.

Jane returns to England and studies ethology, being one of the few people to be allowed to pursue PhD studies without a bachelor degree. After that, her studies are continued with funds from the National Geographic Society. They send a wildlife photographer to document her work; the handsome Dutch nobleman Hugo van Lawick. Like Jane, he has the Sun in Aries. This fiery placement is reinforced by Mars in Sagittarius, sitting right on Jane's Moon and ascendant, and they soon realise they are attracted to each other. Eventually, they marry, which makes Jane a Baroness. Hugo's three planets in Taurus (Mercury, Venus, Uranus), not only make up for Jane's lack in earth, but also activate her 5th house, the house of children.

Looking at Jane's chart, the attention is immediately directed to the Sagittarius Moon on the ascendant. The Moon rules the 8th house, which makes it the key to unlock her unique issues of transformation and self-conquest. The Moon in general also rules motherhood. In her case the square between Moon and Venus/Saturn may bring on certain conflicts between her identity as a woman (Venus) and a mother (Moon). Her own mother, novelist Margaret Myfanwy Joseph (1906–2000), had always supported Jane in pursuing her dreams, particularly when these were traditionally 'male dreams'. Also, Jane had never thought about having children. It just wasn't part of her plan.

Emotional attachments

Different from other scientists at that time, she becomes emotionally attached to the chimps and gives them names. A favourite of hers is Flo, the top ranking female in the community, who later gives birth to a son that Jane names Flint. It is the first time that an infant chimpanzee and the relationship with its mother can be observed so closely in the wild. As a mother, Flo is affectionate, tolerant and nurturing and uses distraction rather than punishment to teach Flint. What Jane admires about Flo is that she is all things a chimp mother should be. She is protective, but not over-protective. The close relationship between her and the chimp family are immensely important for Jane's own development. By becoming closer to animals and nature and being part of all this magic, she also becomes closer to herself. She feels utterly grateful for being accepted by these free, wild animals. Her Moon is square to Neptune in the 9th house, so there is a deep yearning (Moon) to merge (Neptune) with the exotic (9th house). Together with her husband she establishes the Gombe Stream Research Centre in the National Park to extend observations and improve conservation.

Gentle chimps can turn killer

After the death of Flo, who had held the community together, the chimps divide into two separate groups. While one smaller group begins to spend more and more time in a different part of the range, the bigger part of the community stays put. The problem here is that by separating themselves from the main group, these chimpanzees have in a way forfeited their right to be treated as equal community members. By doing this they become strangers, and therefore enemies. This development suddenly turns the hitherto idyllic little paradise upside down. The once so peaceful-seeming chimps now take up a very violent form of primitive warfare and subsequently annihilate all members of the separated group.

This is probably the darkest of times for Jane, because she had always believed that chimpanzees are very similar to humans, only much nicer. She didn't have any idea of the brutality that they can show, when the situation calls for it. Until then, she had always exclusively attributed the capacity for war to humans. Now she has to accept that the darker and more evil side of human nature is also deeply embedded in our genes and inherited from our ancient primate ancestors.

Grub

In 1967, Jane and Hugo have a son, also named Hugo, nicknamed 'Grub'. After having observed so very closely the relationship between Flo and her son Flint, Jane feels that she has learned as much from her positive relationship with her own mother as well as from the chimps. For her son's first three years, Jane isn't separated from him for one single night.

For Grub, growing up in the jungle is a unique experience. No wonder that he, as an adult will return to Africa and work in a resort himself. She teaches him everything she knows, but at one point, he has to go back to the UK for proper schooling. He stays with his grandmother, so the circle comes to a close, in a way. Jane spends holidays with him and tries to see him as often as possible. Having to part with her child because work takes precedence is truly heart-breaking. It goes right under the deeper layers of her 8th house.

In Grub's chart we can trace Jane's maternal sacrifices in the form of the Sagittarius Moon in the 8th as an echo of her Moon as ruler of the 8th. The quincunx with Jupiter at the IC illuminates the joy (8th) of growing up (IC) in total freedom (Jupiter). But the other side of the coin is having to separate from the mother figure in order to follow the values of others. This dynamic causes the native to undergo some serious self-examination in order to find inner emotional resilience. (Moon in the 8th). His inner strength, which will later lead him back to Africa, can also be found in his Scorpio Mars on the descendant. His Jupiter sits on Jane's Pluto and his Saturn on her IC.

In 1974, when Grub is 7, Jane and Hugo divorce. At the end, it became difficult to manage their work and travelling, but they stay on good terms.

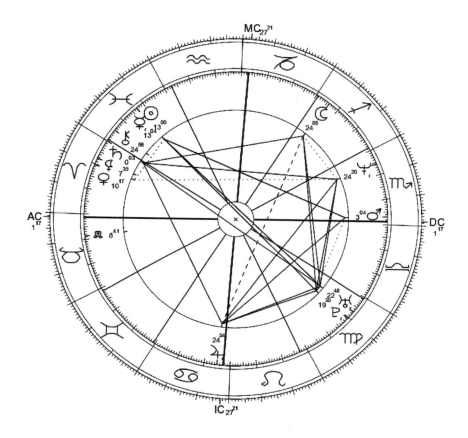

Son: Hugo van Lawick 4 March 1967, 04:00 MSK, Nairobi, Kenya,
RR:AA

8th house constellations

- Moon in Sagittarius in 8th
- Moon square Uranus/Pluto and square Chiron
- Moon at apex of a T-square
- Moon quincunx Jupiter at IC
- Moon ruler of 4th
- Jupiter ruler of 8th
- No air

The following year Jane marries the Director of the national parks, and member of the parliament of Tanzania, Derek Bryceson. Derek, due to his position, can take measures to protect Jane's research project and install an embargo at Gombe. Sadly, Derek dies of cancer in 1980, after five years of marriage. Jane finds solace with her family, friends and spending time in Gombe. Eventually, she overcomes the grief and still stays optimistic, determined and hopeful. In her book *Reason for Hope*, Jane writes that although she had sorrow in her life, she kept her positive and optimistic worldview. Just like in Pandora's Box, at the bottom there is hope.

Impaired face perception

An interesting anecdote is that Jane Goodall suffers from prosopagnosia, also called face blindness, a cognitive disorder of face perception, which impairs the ability to recognize familiar faces, including one's own face (self-recognition), while other aspects of visual processing and intellectual functioning remain intact. (Source: Wikipedia)

I asked my colleague, astrologer Wanda Sellar, if she could find this in Jane's chart, and she came up with some very helpful suggestions. Mercury can be an indicator for neurological diseases, which in Jane Goodall's case is challenged by the opposition with Neptune (nebulousness), a mutual reception, since Mercury is in Pisces and Neptune is in Virgo. The 3rd and 9th houses are linked to the nervous system, mind and brain.

Neptune also squares the Moon on the ascendant (face) and this conjunction is in opposition with Chiron in Gemini in the 6th house of illness. Jupiter rules the ascendant (face) and is placed in Libra (balance) and in opposition to planets in Aries (head) and sits on the Saturn/Neptune midpoint. Venus, the ruler of the 6th house of illness, is in the 3rd house, conjunct Saturn, which in turn rules the 3rd house and squares Chiron. Chiron, however, trines the MC from the 6th house, which indicates a healing talent.

7
Planets in the 8th House

The Sun

The Sun represents the mental, conscious part of our individuality. Its placement in the chart indicates who our role models are and which ideas and principles we identify with. It represents the inner father image, rooted in our childhood. That said, this image needn't necessarily reflect the biological father, because he might have been absent due to various reasons. However, together with Mars, the Sun constitutes the Yang side as far as personal planets are involved.

The Sun in the 8th house might typically come with a certain propensity for feeling melancholy and pensive. In the house of crises and shadows, the father figure is often experienced as detached and self-involved. At the same time, the native might feel that, deep down, he is by no means indifferent. On the contrary, he might very well be emotional and attached, albeit not in an overt manner. This dissonance can account for a certain mistrust in the native's general outlook on life. People might appear aloof, but behind the façade there is always much more going on. In many cases the native might even copy this behaviour or attract people who will also show this demeanour. Also, there is a vague, subtle sort of inner emptiness, a paternal void, if you will. This in turn often leads to a general ambivalence in all areas of life. On the one hand, the native has learned to be content with a minimum of support, comfort and affection. On the other hand, there is a subconscious, slightly nagging feeling of neediness, which now and then might pop up. There is a hunger for intensity in life. One seems to be magically and inexplicably drawn towards the slightest whiff of secrecy, drama, hidden passion and seduction. There is a deep inner need to get recharged. And so, others might be subtly manipulated into giving energy, money, ideas, inspiration, friendship, etc. Under different conditions, this dynamic can also work the other way around, in the form that others might try to tap into the native's energy resources.

This placement may indicate a talent for looking behind other peoples' facades. It can produce excellent researchers, investigators, psychologists or financial administrators. On the flip side of the coin, we might find seducers, manipulators and criminals. Often the native might even be drawn to both sides. Aspects to the Sun will give hints as to whether this placement is of a more constructive or destructive nature; more pleasant or painful. The challenge is to open up to other people and try to find a balance between giving and receiving. Furthermore, one might to try to see the positive side of life and not get dragged down too often.

Sylvia Plath (1932 – 1963), American poet, short story writer and novelist, had Sun in Scorpio in the 8th square Saturn in the 12th and sextile Neptune. Plath is credited with advancing the genre of confessional poetry ('The Bell Jar', 'Ariel'). Her father died when she was eight years old, an emotionally traumatic event which would affect her for the rest of her life. Suffering from clinical depression, she took her own life at the age of thirty. One of her poems is called 'Daddy'.

Betty Ford (1918 – 2011), wife of US president Gerald Ford, confronted two crucial taboos by making public two very sensitive topics. Firstly, that she had to undergo a mastectomy on account of suffering from breast cancer. Secondly, her long-running battle with alcoholism and substance abuse, which required rehabilitation. Afterwards she founded the Betty Ford Centre. A supporter of abortion rights and a leader of the women's movement she was a controversial figure, way ahead of her time. When she was 16 her father died of carbon monoxide poisoning while working under his car, which was understandably very traumatic for the whole family. Her chart has an Aries Sun in the 8th as ruler of the 12th (addictions) trine Saturn/Neptune in the 1st, and a quincunx to Mars in the 1st house.

Moon

The Moon in the chart represents the passive, receiving, instinctive and emotional part of our identity. Its placement indicates what we need to feel secure and at ease. It is strongly connected with childhood memories and our experience with regressive tendencies and maternal issues, which often have their roots in a childhood mother figure.

Moon in the 8th house can indicate that the mother figure had a dominant, albeit somewhat subtle and manipulative influence on the native. In many cases, the mother figure was very assertive and dominant, while not demonstratively cuddly and warm in her affections. Often the native feels that the mother figure was expecting some very specific behaviour and interests from the child, while not allowing others. She could also have had certain ideas about how, specifically, the child is allowed to show emotions, or rather control them. This might have caused the child to suppress and contain vital feelings. Bottled-up feelings always have the tendency to pop up in the form of totally unexpected passionate outbursts, like a pressure cooker, when the lid flies off. In Scorpio, the corresponding sign of the 8th house, the Moon is in the sign of its fall. Emotions and needs are too deeply entangled in the house of shadows, which feels dangerous for the moody luminary. Nevertheless, it is also a placement of great resilience in times of hardship. There is a sort of emotional blockage at work, heavily involved with control issues, neurotically undirected fears, but also jealousy and envy. The challenge is to learn to show and receive softer feelings and allow ambiguity. Furthermore, it can be helpful to realise that in life there is seldom a clear separation between pleasurable and painful emotions, but that they are more often interwoven.

Vivienne Westwood, born 1941, has Moon in Leo in the 8th as ruler of the 8th, trine Sun/Venus in Aries. The eccentric fashion designer likes to shock with her work. She started out from the 1970s punk movement and has ever since been totally devoted to her mission to defy mainstream taste. One of her sons is an erotica photographer, the other the founder of lingerie brand Agent Provocateur. One of her partners was Malcom McLaren, with whom she has a very stormy relationship. She was made a Dame by Queen Elizabeth and is now married to Austrian designer Andreas Kronthaler, who is her junior by 25 years.

Boris Becker, born 1967, has Moon in Cancer as ruler of the 8th in the 8th, opposite Mars, trine Sun/Neptune in the 12th and sextile Pluto in the 9th. The Wimbledon champion was so passionate about playing tennis that he literally missed out on having a normal childhood and adolescence. His mother claims that there was nothing she could do apart from encouraging him. The one-time millionaire has since lost his fortune through bad investments and suffers from serious health problems, such as an enormous tennis elbow.

Mercury

With nosy Mercury in the house of debts, secrets, passions, death and self-conquest we can naturally expect a very inquisitive nature. These natives take an interest in all things extreme, challenging and transformative. This might include the whole 8th house range; finances, manipulation issues, sexuality, the occult or the criminal. They can be confrontational and stick their noses where they don't belong and also are very critical witnesses of every detail around them. This does, by the way, in no way indicate that they open up easily to their environment. On the contrary, these natives tend to be secretive and suspicious. That said, we also have to factor in that Mercury is a very changeable and flexible planet, so aspects and sign give an indication of how the general chart might be affected by this placement.

The English illustrator, author and infamously decadent dandy, **Aubrey Beardsley** (1872 – 1898) had a Mercury/Venus conjunction in Virgo in the 8th, as part of a grand trine with Saturn on his ascendant and Pluto on his IC. In his very short life he emerged as one of the major innovative heads of the Art Nouveau movement. He had a very keen eye for detail and was famous for his witty caricatures and almost pornographic erotic details in his ingenious drawings, which shocked his Victorian contemporaries.

Hungarian-American actor **Bela Lugosi** (1882 – 1956), famous for his portrayal as Count Dracula, on stage and in film, suffered from sciatic neuritis, which was treated with heavy medication and he became addicted to morphine and methadone. His chart displays a Mercury/Mars conjunction in Scorpio in the 8th in a trine with Jupiter in the 4th and a square with the Moon in the 12th.

Venus

Venus is a social planet and indicates everything we fancy and feel attracted to. It reflects the way we try to win others over. Venus in the 8th is in the house of her detriment, since it corresponds with Scorpio. This needn't be an overall negative placement. It does, however, indicate an affinity for unusual aesthetic triggers, such as anything morbid, decayed, tragic and melancholy. Sex is obviously very important here. The native might, if only subconsciously, indulge in the passionate struggle for power in relationships. This Venus, of course largely dependent on her sign, can be infinitely sensuous and seductive, bringing both pleasure and pain in equal parts. Also, money and other manifestations of energy play an important role here. While challenging angles might enhance envy, jealousy, and vindictiveness, harmonious aspects can soften the rough edges and make Venus in the 8th more forgiving and compatible. The challenge is to find a balance between giving and taking, without denying yourself your passionate side.

Margaretha Geertruida Zelle, aka **Mata Hari** (1876 – 1917) had Venus in Cancer in the 8th in opposition with Black Moon Lilith in the 2nd. She tried to live off wealthy men, but was in the end the victim of her narcissism, overconfidence and naivety. The ruler of the 8th, Mercury is part of a stellium in Leo in the 9th (exotic foreign roots, even as a hoax) as apex of a T-square with Jupiter in the 1st (self-presentation) and Pluto in the 7th (public, partners). During WW1 her looks were fading and being short of money she tried to sell herself off to both British and German espionage. Alas, she acted so clumsily that she was caught, brought to trial and shot in 1917.

Jaqueline Kennedy Onassis (1929 – 1994), had a Gemini Venus in the 8th, as ruler of the 7th (spouses), 11th (society) and 12th (behind the scenes) houses, in a trine with the Sun and an opposition with Saturn. She used her feminine demeanour and iconic, elegant glamorous style to camouflage her enormous ambition.

Mars

In classical astrology the 8th house is the natural habitat of Mars, the god of war. This is usually a very passionate placement. It is extremely important to consider sign and aspects in order to find out how this intense kind of energy might materialise. Supportive angles favour the ability to fight for one's passions and relish sexual encounters. Crises are welcomed in order to battle through tough times and be proud afterwards. Challenging placements on the other hand might indicate a suspicious attitude towards life. One might easily feel threatened and act out too excessively and harbour rancour for too long. Mars in the 8th can be a great powerhouse when used wisely.

Impressionist painter **Pierre Auguste Renoir** (1841 – 1919) had Mars in Scorpio in the 8th house as ruler of the 2nd. Mars forms a powerful trine to his Pisces Sun and a sextile to Saturn. A passionate and devoted painter, famous for his appreciation of female beauty, he sadly developed painful arthritis in later life. He developed progressive deformities in his hands and eventually had to have the brush strapped to his paralyzed fingers in order to paint. When asked why he endured this hardship, he said "The pain passes, but the beauty remains." Quote from Wikipedia.

Ronan Farrow (born 1987) son of actor Mia Farrow has a Mars/Pluto conjunction in the 8th in a sextile with Neptune in the 11th house. The *wunderkind* is a human rights activist, journalist, lawyer, and former U.S. government advisor. Although being the legal son of filmmaker Woody Allen, there are rumors that he might in truth be the son of Frank Sinatra, whom he resembles in a most uncanny way. He and his many half-siblings had to endure the dirty custody dispute between his mother and Allen in 1992. Farrow wrote investigative articles for *The New Yorker* which eventually unveiled the Harvey Weinstein sexual abuse allegations. Farrow is openly gay and engaged to podcast host and former presidential speech writer Jon Lovett.

Jupiter

Jupiter indicates where in our chart we have the propensity to feel rich and happy. Jupiter makes every house easier and lighter, even those which are infamous for being troublesome and difficult. In the 8th the native might take any challenges on the chin, staying unperturbed by crises. There is a powerful positive life force at work which always tries to look on the bright side. Also, there is a rare talent for seeing treasures in dark places and potential in seemingly lost causes. Intimate relationships can be very inspiring and joyful. On the downside, expectations might often tend to be unrealistic and the balance of giving and receiving can easily swing to extreme in either direction. A tendency to either give too much and be drained or live off other people's energy resources makes it hard to keep a realistic attitude toward life. Either way, this placement often indicates the ability to overcome hardships like nobody else.

British politician and Member of the House of Commons from 1945 - 1979, **Barbara Castle** (1910 – 2002) had Jupiter in the 8th as part of a stellium and at the base of a T-square with Uranus in the 1st and Neptune in the 7th. She was called "the Margaret Thatcher of the Labour Party". With her flaming red hair and fearless attitude she was a force to be reckoned with. She intervened successfully in the Ford sewing machinists' strike of 1968, in which the women of Dagenham Ford Plant demanded to be paid the same as their male counterparts.

Roger Moore (1927 - 2017) is to me perhaps the sleekest version of James Bond. He made the famous agent come across as very casual and laid back. Moore did have good training in the role of an investigator before taking over Bond from charismatic Sean Connery and difficult George Lazenby, having starred as Simon Templar in the 1960s. While his acting persona was perhaps a bit too polished and good looking, in private he was known to be a very modest and friendly man, never bitching about any of his colleagues and with a marked sense of self-depracation, staying decidedly down-to-earth. His chart shows a retrograde Jupiter in Pisces in a trine with Saturn in Sagittarius in the 4th and quincunx with Sun/Mars in Libra in the 3rd.

Saturn

Saturn, keeper of the threshold, can be experienced in three stages. The first, usually during childhood, is that of repression, when Saturn is experienced in authority figures and rules. The second is compensation, which involves an over-achievement in the native. The third is integration, when one takes responsibility for their own potential to grow via constant self-reflection and patience.

In the 8th house the native might experience the first stage as a general anxiety and inability to trust others. The values of others can be overpowering, leaving little room for self-exploration. The second stage can bring an extreme need to control everything in life. The flow of giving and receiving, so crucial for the 8th house, is stuck. The third stage is often activated through fatal transformative experiences. Loss of control and feeling out of depth are normal and can be accepted without feeling like a total failure.

Also, facing the passionate feelings which the 8th holds in store and which Saturn tries to suppress can alter a person completely and make one much more authentic. The key challenge is always in overcoming one's anxiety.

Austrian-born French Queen **Marie Antoinette** (1755 – 1793), who ended up on the guillotine, had Saturn in Capricorn as ruler of the 8th in the 8th square Moon in Libra in the 5th. She had been for most of her life a vain, superficial and extravagant woman. However, during the revolution, she grew to be an exceptionally brave individual, who showed great inner strength, endured terrible hardships and went to her death unconquered. A perfect example of how the planet of maturity, often one-dimensionally perceived as restricting and cold, can shine in times of crisis, bringing out hidden talents in the native.

Lyndon Baines Johnson (1908 - 1973), is one of the most underestimated presidents of the USA of all time. His chart shows a retrograde Saturn in Aries as the apex of a T-square with Uranus in the 5th and Venus/ Neptune in the 11th. He had the bad luck to follow the hugely popular

Kennedy in 1964, and live through the Vietnam war, which grew into a national disaster. On the other hand, under his legislation he supported civil rights, public broadcasting and medicare. He had an erratic streak, was domineering and known for the 'Johnson treatment', meaning that he would cross any boundaries, both physically and politically. He also had a long-time mistress and an illegitimate son.

Chiron

Chiron indicates where in the chart our deepest and most intimate wound is. It is our Achilles heel. Animals lick their wounds. And so, symbolically, we humans have to do the same. This means taking very good care of ourselves, staying alert and protective, introspective and empathic. And although childhood wounds will never heal completely, we really need to feel them now and then. Where Chiron is, we will always stay vulnerable. This can be a powerful gift, a mighty potential in terms of feeling compassion, for ourselves as well as for others. When we learn to open up and share our pain with others who might suffer from a similar pain, the effect can be very soothing. That is why Chiron is called 'the wounded healer'.

In the 8th house the wound can be of a sexual nature, or the native has been otherwise traumatised as a child, or subtly suffering from a feeling of being deeply scared. It also touches issues around death, debts and secrets, as well as taboos. Like in the other two water houses, Chiron feels particularly emotional here. Since this is the house of intimate relationships, we look for someone to share our pain with. But this person needs to open up as well. Only by building up trust in each other, we can feel the pain and let it go again. And again, and again...

In the chart of actor **Kevin Spacey**, born 1959, the Aquarius Chiron is retrograde in the 8th house as apex of a T-square with Black Moon Lilith in Taurus in the 11th and Jupiter in Scorpio in the 4th. In 2017 the successful star and much-acclaimed character actor (*House of Cards*) was publicly accused of sexual misconduct with underage men. The result was he was sacked by Netflix and cut out of the film *All the Money in the World* about billionaire Paul Getty. He retired from public life for over a year and has since returned to defend his reputation.

Martin Luther (1483 – 1546), German professor of theology, priest, monk and seminal figure in the Protestant Reformation had a Pisces Chiron in the 8th, trine Sun in Scorpio in the 4th and quincunx Jupiter in the 3rd. Luther was passionately opposed to the concept of indulgence trade and believed that every Christian could feel God's presence directly through prayer without a priest, which was anathema for the Roman Catholic Church. His translation of the Bible into German made it more accessible for the genereal public. He was eventually excommunicated by the Pope and condemned as an outlaw by the Holy Roman Emporor.

Uranus

The house in which Uranus is placed is often subject to fluctuations and sudden changes. To deal with this, one has to stay very flexible and inventive. The 8th house is a place of fixed water and can be either very rigid or very passionate. It is also a house of self-conquest and transformation. Uranus, as an air planet, in the 8th is very challenging, since it feels a bit on foreign territory in a water house. It is a planet of distance rather than of emotional intimacy, therefore producing a good deal of ambivalence. So it could be that the native feels drawn towards very eccentric and original individuals. Furthermore, the nervous, unpredictable nature of the planet can cause extreme variations between hot and cold, like a rollercoaster. Sexual encounters can also be thrilling and unconventional. That said, double-bind messages and endless games of hide and seek might make serious relationships difficult. The solution is to keep each other on a long leash and try not to be possessive and jealous. Dealing with money could also be taxing, because the native might have difficulties grasping the conventional concept of contracts or taxes.

The astrologer **Richard Idemon** (1938 – 1985) had a Taurus Uranus in the 8th as ruler of the 5th house with squares to Sun/Venus, Mercury and Jupiter, all in Aquarius. He was particularly interested in depth psychology and the astrological patterns of relationships. He had an unconventional and very passionate approach and also taught astrology in prisons. His books *Through the Looking Glass* and *The Magic Thread* brought me endless hours of inspiration and entertainment.

The divine **Greta Garbo** (1905 – 1990) had Uranus at the critical degree of 0° Capricorn in the 8th as ruler of the 11th house in a T-square with her Virgo Sun in the 6th as apex and opposite Pluto. Although she had a couple of passionate love affairs with men and women, she preferred to stay single for most of her life. After she retired from film at age 36 she withdrew more and more, protecting her privacy with a reticence that was almost pathological. However, she enjoyed the company of friends and lived high up in an exquisitely decorated apartment in a New York skyscraper, very appropriate for Uranus.

Neptune

Neptune represents the part of us which is longing to merge with something or someone. The most fascinating of the planets, it is very difficult to pin down since it changes constantly. It is about symbiosis, seeking inspiration and romance, but also a propensity for getting lost. Neptune wants everything easy and dreamy. In a positive way, its placement can indicate where we are romantic, artistic and altruistic. In a more detrimental way, it may be a place of deception, where we tend to over-idolise, feel weak, victimised and become addicted.

In the 8th house, depending on its aspects, Neptune can mean that we devote ourselves to a partner with whose values we might merge selflessly and altruistically. But then we might also lose all sense of self-awareness or our material possessions. Neptune is not at all a materialistic planet and doesn't care about money, unless it can be used to buy nice things or to make life easier. The 8th house is a very intimate place. With Neptune here, sex can be very inventive and joyous. Furthermore, there might be a tendency to attract people in need, which might make it difficult to see people and financial matters objectively. There might be a tendency to create myths and lies, albeit not necessarily in bad faith. Since Neptune likes to play, act out and deceive, one should be always be on guard when dealing with these natives.

Jules Verne (1825 – 1905), is a very creative and visionary example who, with Neptune as the head of a kite in the 8th house, was one of the first science fiction novelists. *Journey to the Centre of the Earth*, and *20,000 Leagues Under the Sea* perfectly reflect the yearning to dive deep and explore the mysteriously hidden 'underworld'.

The discovery chart of Neptune (24 September 1846, see detailed chart at www.astro.com) displays a tight Neptune/Uranus conjunction in the 8th. It forms a quincunx with Mars in the 3rd and a sextile with Pluto in the 10th, making it a yod, with Mars as the apex.

The time of the discovery was an extremely chaotic one, with many social and spiritual problems. Neptune in the 8th here shows the growing uncertainty of which sort of values actually counted for humanity in a time of great change.

Pluto

This is the natural habitat of Pluto, ruler of the underworld, and renders the perfect background for his calling to execute total power, giving the native resilience and courage. This might be applicable in all typical 8th house affairs, such as sexuality, values of others, death, border sciences, confrontation, taboos and border crossings. Challenging aspects, however, might indicate that the native has to struggle much harder to achieve goals than others. Entanglements, intrigues and passionate stubbornness might bring one into collision with enemies. Harmonious angles, on the other hand, might support a more agreeable attitude. Like Mars in the 8th, this placement can be associated with the last man standing on the battlefield, with even stronger willingness to conquer and transform. Many natives, however, might remain unaware of this hidden source of strength, unless opportunity calls in times of need and hardship.

Angela Merkel, Germany's first female chancellor was born 1954, survived many hardships during her long career and is well-known for her calm demeanour in times of crisis and for outliving many national and international politicians. Her chart shows Pluto in the 8th in opposition to Moon in Aquarius in the 2nd house and sextile to Neptune at the MC. This might account for her unemotional and somewhat cold attitude and her total devotion to her role.

Astronomer **Galileo Galilei's** (1564 – 1642) vehement championing of heliocentrism brought him into confrontation with the Roman Inquisition, which found him guilty of heresy and put him under house arrest for the last 10 years of his life. His 8th house displays a prominent Pluto placement in a stellium with the Sun, Mercury and Venus in Pisces as the apex of a T-square with Mars and Uranus. Neptune, ruler of the 8th, is in the 10th, showing how breaking taboos and sticking to his convictions (8th) was part of his calling (10th).

South Node

With the South Node in the 8th house, the native is often fascinated with taboos, secrets and the darker sides of life. Other people's boundaries are not always respected, causing a lot of discomfort. There is a deep feeling of mistrust combined with the urge to dig deep to unveil hidden motives. While one might appear strong and self-confident, there is a deep mistrust and helplessness underneath. Since this is the South Node, the task in life is to leave the shores of the 8th and swim towards the more reassuring shores of the 2nd house. It's true, everything in life has to die, but isn't it also true that every moment is precious and can be treasured? This is not easy, because it requires a willingness to embrace the inner sources of self-esteem. These are often overshadowed by the belief that life might always interfere by pulling the rug from under one's feet. Trust is the key word here. It can be helpful to connect more and more with the sensuous aspects in life. The second house corresponds with Taurus, the sign of of earthly pleasures and reassurance. Feeling the beauty of nature and the joy of sexuality are treasures to discover. In many ways, this journey is one of the hardest, since it requires us to let go of negative experience and distrust.

Edward, Duke of Windsor (1894 – 1972) had the South Node in the 8th in Libra. His father, George V, was a cruel parent, while his mother, Queen Mary, was submissive and couldn't protect her children against her husband. Never good enough in the eyes of his father, Edward found his duties as heir to the throne extremely tiresome. In 1936, at the age of 42, after having been king for less than a year, he abdicated. The values of others (8th), in his case came in the form of the demand that he broke off his plan to marry the twice divorced American socialite Wallis Simpson. This would have been a scandal to the British establishment and Anglican Church, although many of his subjects sympathised with him. For the rest of his life, he led a life of pleasure (2nd house), albeit somewhat shallow, since he didn't have a concrete role anymore. His Sun in Cancer forms a stressful square to the nodes, which symbolizes his great sacrifice. He had to leave his country and family (Cancer) in order to break free and fight for his right to choose a wife (North Node in Aries in the 2nd). They were married in France in 1937; none of the Royal family attended the function, and his brother, the new king, refused to grand Wallis the title of HRH.

North Node

With the North Node in the 8th house the native is often drawn into the dramas of life. While past lives might have been spent around matters of the 2nd house, such as planting something lasting, the current incarnation demands to let go. This is by no means an easy task. One needs a lot of courage to face the unknown dangers of being entangled in the intimacy of relationships and plans. The clue here can be the inner certainty that, while nothing ever stays the same, there is always an inner strength and resilience. Sexuality can become a vital part in experiencing the boundaries within human interaction. By coming closer and closer to the edge, one realises how precious life is.

The directing work of jack-of-all-trades artist **David Lynch**, born 1946, includes classics such as *Blue Velvet*, *The Elephant Man* and *Lost Highway*. In his films he often tries to unveil the dark side of human behaviour and creates a very special brand of sinister, nightmarish, yet sexy atmosphere, loaded with tension. In his chart the North Node in Gemini in the 8th forms a trine with Jupiter in the 11th. Lynch practises Transcendental Meditation in order to bring peace to the world. The following quote I find particularly fitting for the 8th house:

> *We're all like detectives in life. There's something at the end of the trail that we're all looking for.*
> (Quote from Wikipedia)

Black Moon Lilith

Black Moon Lilith is not a planet, but a sensitive point on the Moon's elliptical orbit which is the furthest away from the earth. Not all astrologers attach a great deal of significance to it, but I like to include it in my interpretations because I often find that it can shed light on gender role issues. It has to do with matters of emancipation, when certain facets of femininity are rejected by the patriarchal order.

In the 8th house, the place of taboos, sexuality and transformation, Lilith can indicate a keen interest in challenging feminine power issues and confronting the world with surprising and unconventional ways to live out one's Yin side. The Lilith myth in the Kabbalah has it that Lilith, first wife of Adam in the Garden of Eden, wanted to lie on top rather than oblige her partner by getting into the rule-book missionary position. In the 8th it might feel particularly hard to suppress any urges to free oneself from what men in society, family and partnerships expect from you. This might also hold true for rejected Yin sides in a man. So, while women might find themselves criticised for being threateningly strong as females, men experience similar rejection for showing 'unmanly' and epicene soft sides. Since the 8th is a fearless place of self-conquest, these natives won't budge easily. However, it often requires an extreme situation, when finding oneself being pushed too hard, before the native unleashes his or her inner powerful female side.

Gay fashion designer **Lee Alexander McQueen** (1969 - 2010), boldly challenged perceptions of femininity by his sexy, provocative and morbid clothes. He invented low-cut trousers and created bustiers, using sculls and moths (both 8th house symbols) in his designs. McQueen often shocked audiences with his innovatively extravagant catwalk shows. His collections revealingly sported names as 'Savage Beauty' or 'Plato's Atlantis'. McQueen was very close to his mother. Shortly after her death in February 2010, he committed suicide, having suffered from mixed anxiety and depressive disorder and drug abuse. Apart from Scorpio rising and an opposition between his Sun/Moon conjunction in Pisces in the 5th with Pluto in the 11th, his chart displays a marked Lilith on the apex of a T-square with Chiron and Jupiter/Uranus.

8

8th House Rulership Combinations

The 12 houses in the chart represent 12 different areas of life. These areas coexist and influence each other according to the relationships of their house rulers. For example: the way we approach encounters and partnerships (7th house) might strongly depend on our ability to overcome inner fears (8th house), when these houses are connected by rulership. The cusp of a house always falls into a specific sign.

Each sign is ruled by a specific planet, which is then called the ruler. Let's assume that the cusp of the 5th house falls into Sagittarius. The ruler of Sagittarius is Jupiter. Now let's assume that in our example Jupiter is in the 1st house. The equation would be: ruler of the 5th house is in the 1st house. But what does this mean? The house which is ruled by a particular planet is the place where its inner motives lie. These motives are carried to the house in which the planet is placed. Decoding these relationships makes the chart much more vivid and complex.

So, in our little example, we might deduce that Jupiter brings its motives from the 5th house into the 1st house. The 5th house is the place of self-presenting, joy, play and zest for life, as well as creativity and children. The 1st house shows how we approach life and how we come across spontaneously. Both houses are fire houses, dealing with the ego. In this case, the native might show a certain degree of self-confidence and come across as a force to be reckoned with. This of course must be further supported by other placements in the chart. If we have, let's say Scorpio or Cancer rising, this energy might be a bit less obvious.

Classical or modern ruler?

Over the last few years there has been a harmonisation between the often rather divided classical and modern astrology schools. From my point of view, you can use both schools, given that both have their particular strengths. For example, it is possible to use the classical rulership system which works with only 7 planets when looking at the consultation chart, and later have a more analytical look at the birth chart with the rules of modern psychological astrology. I find that most astrologers tend use one school more than the other. When dealing with rulers, this is of course crucial. Looking at Aquarius, does one work with its classical ruler Saturn or its modern ruler Uranus? Is the classical ruler Jupiter responsible for Pisces or the modern ruler Neptune? Does Mars or Pluto rule Scorpio? My advice is to stay open-minded, but on the other hand not jump too often from one school to the other, otherwise it will only end up in confusion. I myself always work with the modern rulers when dealing with birth charts.

Collective or individual ruler?

In an idealised chart with whole sign houses, the ascendant always is at 0° Aries. It naturally follows the 8th house cusp is at 0° Scorpio, its ruler always being Mars or Pluto. In an individual chart the cusps of the houses could fall into any sign at any degree. Since I know of astrologers who work with collective rulers for the houses, I must mention that I work with Placidus and thus with individual rulership.

Intercepted signs

Since I don't work with whole sign houses, but with Placidus, many charts display houses with unequal sizes. Often one is confronted with very small houses, where several cusps can fall into the same sign. On the other hand, this means that other signs are intercepted, meaning that they have no house cusps. In the latter case a house would have more than one ruler. The main ruler is always the one ruling the sign of the cusp. The co-ruler is the ruler of the intercepted sign. This ruler is by no means unconnected; it just has a more downbeat and subliminal influence.

Obviously, not every chart displays a planet in the 8th house, but it always has a ruler of the 8th house, according to the sign on the cusp. And the house in which this ruler is placed does give further information about the native's inner 8th house motives.

Ruler of the 8th house

The house in which the ruler of the 8th house falls is a place where one might feel the subtle effects of a hidden agenda of passion, entanglement and the values of others. In this house we often feel inexplicably intense and passionate.

Planets in the 8th house as house rulers

Any planet which is placed in the 8th house carries, as ruler of its house or houses, a particular agenda with it. In the 8th the planet unconsciously seeks confrontation with the native's inner passions and suppressed feelings, with matters of life and death and self-conquest.

8th house rulership combinations
Ruler of 8th in 1st

Not dissimilar to Pluto in the 1st or Scorpio rising, this combination might indicate a charismatic and yet mysterious personality. One might feel somewhat ambivalent in the presence of these natives. Getting to know them requires a lot of courage and endurance. While they might bring out your innermost secrets, they themselves remain unnervingly non-committal. This is a great placement for anyone who wants to check out circumstances and opportunities, like a detective or therapist. These natives can put you to the acid test. But if you have survived all their secret games, they will stay with you come what may. Since the 8th is the house of crises, their lives are often a real rollercoaster.

Theo van Gogh (1857 – 1891), brother of famous painter Vincent, had Pluto as ruler of the 8th in his 1st house, square the Moon in the 5th house. He was a successful art dealer who supported his beloved, but difficult brother both financially and morally. He also had Mercury as ruler of the 3rd (siblings) in a stellium in the 2nd house of finances. His brother's death caused Theo to become deeply apathetic and he passed away in a mental institution just six months later.

Woody Allen, born 1935; the famous director, comedian and actor is also infamous for his difficult relationship with actress Mia Farrow and his affair with their adoptive daughter, Soon-Yi, whom he later married. He has had very bad press regarding accusations of pedophelia, since this relationship with Soon-Yin might have begun when she was still a minor. In his chart Neptune as ruler of the 8th in the 1st house receives a trine from Mars in Capricorn in the 5th and squares from the Sun, Mercury and Jupiter in the 4th house.

Marilyn Monroe (1926 – 1962) had Neptune as ruler of the 8th in the 1st house with a Pisces Mars in the 8th, both entangled in a challenging quincunx. She used her unique brand of highly-charged eroticism, which was non-threatening and child-like, to fuel her career. Her persona served millions of admirers as a projection screen (Neptune in the 1st). Although she herself enjoyed sex, she realised too late that she had become the victim of her own, self-created image of a seductress, while what she really craved was being respected for her acting talents. The combination of the planet Neptune and a planet in Pisces in a challenging aspect strongly suggests that there is a thin line between creating an illusion and becoming the victim of it.

Ruler of 1st in 8th

This constellation often indicates a confrontational, albeit cautious and very profound way of approaching life. The native is strongly driven by instinct and not easy to read. With the ruler of the 1st in the 8th one often experiences all facets of life in the extreme. It often goes hand in hand with an inquisitive mind and a curiosity for intense encounters. This may explain why so many natives with this placement seem to live life on the edge. Letting go, on the other hand, may be difficult for these sometimes extreme control-freaks.

Brigitte Macron, born 1953, the wife of President Emmanuel Macron, met her future husband, who is almost 25 years her junior, when she was his teacher. They fell in love and married. In her chart Mercury in Pisces is the ruler of the 1st house as part of a yod figure with quincunx Saturn/Neptune in the 3rd as apex and sextile Jupiter on the MC. A considerably older woman paired with a younger man is still taboo.

Legendary pop icon **David Bowie** (1947 – 2016) was known for reinventing himself again and again with different personas and experimenting with drugs. While he toyed around with bisexuality he was in reality heterosexual and extremely devoted to his partners, especially his wives Angela and Imam. His chart displays Neptune as co-ruler of the 1st house (Aquarius rising, and Pisces intercepted) in the 8th, trine Uranus in the 5th, sextile Pluto in the 7th and square Sun/Mars in Capricorn in the 12th. So toying around with his public persona while grounding himself in real-life relationships seemed a perfect combination. It certainly worked for Bowie, who had a reputation of being down-to-earth and very sympathetic.

Ruler of 8th in 2nd

These houses are naturally contradictory. Fixed earth meets fixed water. Earth needs constancy; water is the element of change and flexibility. With this combination the values of others have a strong impact on the values of the chart owner. A partnership with obsessive undercurrents or fixations can have considerable influence on our own self-esteem, which might bring intense ups and downs. A real roller-coaster. Also, the native's talents could be strongly influenced by the resources of others. So there is a struggle for self-confidence, which will grow by overcoming all sorts of odds. There might also be taboos and hidden psychological agendas at work. Since the 2nd house is also the place of pleasure and sensuality there is often an underlying passion, which can also swing to a more painful side.

Mohammed Ali (1942 – 2016) had Neptune retrograde in the 2nd as ruler of the 8th house at the critical degree of 29° Virgo as part of a grand trine with Saturn/Uranus in the 10th and a Scorpio Sun in the 6th. He had no water in his chart. He wasn't only a champion boxer but saw himself as a showman, referring to himself as 'the Greatest'. He changed his name from Cassius Clay when he became a Muslim. He was known as someone who was deeply dedicated to his goals and beliefs. Drastic changes in values can be typical for this placement.

Diana, Princess of Wales (1961 – 1997) had an Aquarius Moon in the 2nd house as ruler of the 8th as part of a T-square, with the apex Venus in the 5th and opposition Uranus in the 8th. Her 8th house also contained Mars, Pluto, Black Moon Lilith and the North Node. Idolised by the public and haunted by the press, she soon began to feel trapped in her unhappy marriage to Prince Charles. Emotionally unstable and needy, she developed anorexia due to the pressures that came with her position. After her tragic death at age 36 she was mythologized as a victim. This isn't really true. She was nobody's fool and knew how to use the press to her advantage. Some argue that she suffered from a possibly borderline personality disorder.

Ruler of 2nd in 8th

This combination gives the native greater influence than the 8th in 2nd placement. The native tries to influence the values of others and experiences intense encounters. These natives are often very charismatic, albeit unconsciously and unintentionally. The 8th house is often out of balance, so their own values might be subject to fluctuations as well. Since the 2nd house deals with matters of security and self-worth, it is daring and takes guts to look for help in the 8th house of crises and self-conquest. Life might challenge you rather more often when it comes to transforming values and self-concepts. Deep down there is a burning yearning for extreme encounters and to push boundaries. Superficial small talk or polite polish quickly becomes boring.

In the chart of **Kaia Gerber,** born 2001, daughter of supermodel Cindy Crawford, a Cancer Jupiter in the 8th is the ruler of the 2nd house with a quincunx to Pluto in the 1st house and a sextile to her Virgo Sun in the 10th. She started out as a child model and is now almost as successful as her mother used to be. Her appeal is a mixture of aloofness and sex appeal; a perfect projection screen for the postmodern glamour world where youth is valued more than ever.

Harry Houdini (1874 – 1926), the Hungarian-born illusionist and stunt performer, who was famous for his escape acts (often under water), had a Sun/Venus conjunction in the 2nd house, with Venus being the ruler of the 8th house. Venus forms a sextile with Uranus on the descendant and a trine with Saturn on the ascendant. The ability to elegantly (Venus) ascend (Hellenistic interpretation of the 2nd house) from the underworld (8th house) and release himself from chains (Saturn opposition Uranus) was totally ingenious.

Ruler of 8th in 3rd

The 3rd house is a mutable air house and encompasses the areas of learning, networking, short journeys, but also gossip, siblings and neighbours. It is also referred to as the market place in the chart and can serve as a lively background for any planet that is placed here, almost like in a beehive. But when the ruler of the 8th house, with its forceful energy, is placed in the 3rd, then superficiality and flightiness haven't got a chance anymore. Any planet that serves as ruler of the 8th house might bring passion and ambition in this house. Small talk? No, thank you, not interested. This constellation strongly supports thinking, communication and networking. But only for one aim: in-depth exchange to get to the heart of the matter, even if it means confrontation and overstepping boundaries. These natives can have a compelling influence on their environment. It is very hard to resist this charismatic force. And so, one might give away intimate details or gossip without having learned anything at all from the native. Siblings and neighbours might also play an important role by serving as a mirror of one's own power struggles.

Karl Marx (1818 - 1883), the German-Jewish communist and philosopher who developed the theory of socialism and wrote *Das Kapital*, had Venus in Taurus as ruler of the 8th in the 3rd with a sextile to Saturn in the 1st and quincunxes to retrograde Neptune/Uranus in Sagittarius in the 10th. Marx was a prolific writer but suffered from ill health and poor income for most of his life, which didn't stop him from working.

Austrian neurologist and psychiatrist **Alfred Adler** (1870 – 1937) had an Aquarius Sun in the 8th as ruler of the 2nd and 3rd house with a quincunx to Uranus in the 1st and a square to a Moon/Jupiter/Pluto conjunction in Taurus in the 11th. He elaborated on the importance of the social element in re-adjustment development of the individual. He also came up with new insights about the inferiority complex.

Ruler of 3rd in 8th

This position can indicate that the exchange of information in everyday life tends to have a confrontational nature, like 'a dog with a bone'. Networking might strongly involve the values of others or taboos and is dealt with in a subtle, hidden, enigmatic way. However, this passionate inquisitiveness might be subconscious. The goal is to shed light on hidden agendas and to seek transformation. The native likes to play with boundaries and might conspire to create crises. It might be a good combination for a detective or a therapist.

Wladimir Iljitsch Lenin (1870 – 1924) had Uranus in the 8th as ruler of the 3rd, square Mars in Aries in the 5th and trine Venus in Pisces in the 3rd. Lenin was one of history's great agitators and tyrants who, in 1917, caused the so-called October Revolution in Russia.

In the chart of Labour politician **Jeremy Corbyn**, born 1949, a Gemini Uranus at the critical degree of 29° rules the 2nd house and is part of a yod figure with quincunx Jupiter retrograde in the 2nd and a sextile with Saturn in Leo also at the critical degree of 29°. Corbyn polarises as a public figure. While some are charmed by his charisma and natural way with people, others despair of his indecisiveness.

Ruler of 8th in 4th

With this constellation there is often a yearning to find peace by coming to terms with childhood matters. Also, any partner can potentially become an intimate soulmate and part of the family. These characters take nothing for granted and don't fear moral or financial hardships. Home, ancestry and family are values worth fighting for.

Alexandria Ocasio-Cortez, born 1989, has Moon on the IC as ruler of the 8th, in opposition to Mercury, square Jupiter in the 8th, square Uranus in the 1st and trine Venus in the 12th. Ocasio-Cortez is an American politician, activist and representative (Democrat) for New York's 14th congressional district. The daughter of poor Puerto Ricans, she fought her way into politics with hardly any financial funds at all and represents a new generation of courageous female politicians. Her much-adored father, who died prematurely, once showed the young girl the House of Congress in Washington and told her: 'This belongs to all of us, and you too.'

King Henry VIII (1491 – 1547) had a Sagittarius Neptune as ruler of the 8th in the 4th house as part of a T-square with apex Mars in Virgo in the 1st and opposition Jupiter in Gemini in the 10th house. When Henry fell in love with Anne Boleyn and wanted to marry her, the Pope refused to annul his marriage with Queen Catherine of Aragon. In order to impose his will, Henry cut England off the Roman Catholic Church and made himself head of the newly founded Church of England. While the King in his youth was good looking, courteous, warm-tempered and generous, he became unpredictable and moody in later years because of ill health, and had two of his six wives beheaded.

Ruler of 4th in 8th

Like 8th in 4th, the combination 4 and 8 also signifies deep psychological self-exploration since both are water houses. The 4th house deals with childhood, heritage, roots, family and soul-searching. When its ruler is found in the 8th house these issues are often hard to experience and might undergo several crises before finding peace. These natives are anything but superficial and seek real companionship and a life of passion. Pain and suffering don't scare them when they are involved.

Peter Townsend (1914 – 1995), had Neptune as ruler of the 4th in the 8th, trine Sun in Scorpio in the 12th, opposite the Moon, square Mercury in the 12th. Townsend was a Royal Air Force pilot and equerry to King

George VI. After the king's death in 1952 he was romantically involved with Princess Margaret, who was 16 years his junior and who found in him stability. She was forbidden to marry the divorced Townsend because of royal protocol. He later became an author.

Jack London (1876 – 1916), the American novelist (*The Call of the Wild*), journalist, activist and early innovator of science fiction had his Capricorn Sun in the 8th as ruler of the 4th house and apex of a small talent triangle and square Neptune in the 12th. The ruler of the 8th house, Saturn, was extremely challenged on the MC with a Venus conjunction, opposition Moon/Uranus and squares with Jupiter in the 4th and Pluto in the 12th. During his relatively short life, the son of an astrologer was under constant pressure and suffered from a multitude of illnesses. He finally died of an overdose of morphine.

Ruler of 8th in 5th

This placement combines two very passionate houses, both fixed in modality, and water and fire also always make a very heartfelt and sometimes frenzied mix. As both houses form a natural square, the water side and the fire side can easily be in conflict with each other. Fixed water is controlled and seeks intense encounters. Fixed fire is all about self-presentation and having fun. This clashes as soon as the chart-owner leaves superficial flirting behind and starts to feel something deeper. Games can reach a point when suddenly other issues are at stake. Children might become an unexpected challenge. In any case, what makes this placement an odd one is the element of unexpected change in pace and intensity. Crises are absolutely unavoidable, but, when battled through, leave the chart-owner with replenished strength and authenticity.

The Austrian politician **Sebastian Kurz,** born 1986, has a retrograde Pisces Jupiter in the 8th as ruler of the 5th house, square Uranus in the 5th and quincunx Venus in Libra in the 3rd house. He also has the ruler of the 8th house, Neptune, in the 5th house, sextile Pluto on the IC and trine Mercury in the 1st house. Both charming and ambitious, he became the youngest Minister of Foreign Affairs in European history at age 27. Later, during his time as chancellor of Austria from 2017 till 2019, he was involved in many scandals and finally forced to resign after a motion of no confidence. However, he is expected to come back again and play an important role in politics.

Princess Margaret Rose (1930 – 2002) had a Cancer Pluto as ruler of the 8th house in the 5th, conjunct the Moon and as apex of a T-square with Uranus in Aries in the 1st and Venus in Libra in the 7th house. As the younger sister of Queen Elizabeth II, she often felt the mere second fiddle, although many thought her the brighter and more beautiful of the two. Being forbidden by royal protocol to marry Peter Townsend, she had to wait until she was 30 years-old before she finally married the society photographer Lord Anthony Snowdon. During her whole life she was never quite sure who she wanted to be. Sometimes she insisted upon living free and unrestricted. At other times she behaved more royal than any other member of her family, insisting on deference and keeping people at a distance. During the 1950s and 60s she was one of the most glamorous women and treated almost like a film star.

Ruler of 5th in 8th

This pairing is as intense as the combination of 8th in 5th. This combination is about seeking self-confrontation via playing, self-presentation and creativity. It also can involve children. The normally rather joyous energy of the 5th house, which has natural analogies with the self-loving Leo sign, is tinted in a darker hue when its ruler is placed in the 8th and feels much more serious. The chart-owner is anxious to show the world who he or she is. But this might not come naturally. Instead one has to conquer a lot of fears. Often control and mistrust can be issues. One has very passionate relationships with children, but also products of one's own creativity. Since both the 5th and 8th houses involve erotic and romantic issues, and flirting can become a means of manipulation. A latent danger can also be a tendency to gambling compulsiveness and being too easily in debt.

George, Prince of Cambridge, born 2013, eldest son of Prince William, has a very full 8th house with the Sun at the last degree of Cancer and a grand stellium of Mercury, Mars, Jupiter and Black Moon Lilith also in Cancer. Mars is the ruler of the 5th house and part of a grand trine with Saturn in Scorpio in the 11th and Neptune in Pisces in the 4th. Mars is also part of a T-square with apex Uranus in the 5th and an opposition with Pluto in the 2nd house. Since he is third in line to succeed the throne after his grandfather and father, it is quite realistic to assume that he will someday be king. This must naturally come with a lot of responsibility and ability to adapt to the zeitgeist on the one hand and tradition on the other hand. Looking at the T-square with apex Uranus in the 5th this seems quite a challenge, even now.

Marion March (1923 – 2001), German-American astrologer who also has the ruler of the 3rd house in the 8th involved in a great trine and a T-square in her chart, in her case Neptune. The planet of yearning forms an opposition to her Aquarius Sun in the 2nd and a square with Jupiter in the 11th. The two trines are with Mars in Aries on the IC and Moon in Sagittarius on the ascendant. She spoke several languages and lived in many countries before settling down. One of the most renowned astrologers in the world, she co-authored the best-selling series *The Only Way to Learn Astrology* (1980).

Ruler of 8th in 6th

The 6th and the 8th houses are both critical and analytical. Both being in natural quincunx to the ascendant, they are often experienced as strenuous. With the ruler of the 8th in the 6th the chart-owner is normally challenged to face his or her crises and problems arising out of closer relationships in everyday life, working them off, so to speak. This requires a certain degree of stoicism and determination. The areas of household routines, diet, work and health are approached with seriousness, bordering on obsession. Ironically this level of intensity doesn't necessarily feel burdensome, but rather normal. With each mastered crisis, often accompanied by psychosomatic symptoms, one becomes more and more able and self-confident. Since the 6th house is also the house of service, one is often excellently qualified for many lines of work, which involve devotion and stamina.

In the chart of **Johannes Kepler** (1571 – 1630), the German astrologer, astronomer and mathematician, we find Saturn in Scorpio in the 6th as ruler of the 8th, sextile the Sun and Venus in the 8th and trine Jupiter in the 11th. Kepler discovered three major laws of planetary motion, working obsessively and against many odds. He looked down on trivial astrology and rather regarded astrology as something divine and serious, using it not only for consultation, but also for introspection and self-awareness.

Claus von Stauffenberg (1907 – 1944), German officer in WWII, had Mars in Aquarius in the 6th as ruler of the 8th, as part of a T-square with an opposition to Jupiter in the 12th and square Sun/Mercury in Scorpio in the 3rd. Stauffenberg was one of the leading members of the failed 1944 plot to assassinate Hitler and was executed.

Ruler of 6th in 8th

This combination is more enigmatic than the placement of 8th in 6th. Work, health, service and every day affairs can more easily result in passionate entanglements, financial challenges and other personal crises. Life is a struggle and we must learn to battle through. There is also a deep need for control and power. People with this placement are often very resilient and fearless and inspired by an insatiable curiosity and urge to test all sorts of boundaries. Once hooked, they are very hard to get rid of, like a dog with a bone. This is an excellent placement for psychology, crime and crime fighting, but also for dealing with financial affairs

Italian-American journalist **Gay Talese**, born 1932, has an Aries Uranus conjunct Black Moon Lilith in the 8th house as ruler of the 6th house with a square to Pluto in the 11th, a sextile with Sun/Mars in Aquarius in the 6th and a trine with Jupiter in the 12th house. Since Mars is the ruler of his 8th house, he has the 6th and the 8th in a dual rulership relationship, making this combination significant. Talese cuts an eccentric dandy figure and dresses impeccably even in old age. He still loves to work without any distraction in the basement of his Manhattan house. His work includes *Thy Neighbour's Wife*, an exploration of sexuality in America with a discussion of a free love subculture. To gain insight he spent several months in a nudist resort. He also wrote *The Voyeur's Motel*, the utterly weird but nonetheless true story of a Peeping Tom motel owner who spent years watching his guests via holes in the ceiling of their rooms.

German politician **Walter Ulbricht** (1893 – 1973), leader of East Germany from 1950 – 1971, had Neptune conjunct Pluto in Gemini in the 8th house as ruler of the 6th house, trine Saturn in the 12th. He was infamous for lying to the press that the government had 'no intention whatsoever to build a wall'. Soon after this, the Berlin wall was built after all. Ulbricht, a ruthless power-monger, was probably the most hated figure in the East German communist government. He was disposed of by a coup and replaced by Erich Honecker, who wasn't significantly more popular.

Ruler of 7th in 8th

The 7th house deals with encounters, the public and partnership. In the 8th house we go further and enter the realm of entanglement and intimate relationships. The 8th is the house of taboos, sexuality and self-conquest. It is also a place in the chart where we have specific ideas of how things in life should be. With this combination we are looking for someone with whom we can really grow spiritually and morally. This invites confrontations and friction. Intensive encounters can be deeply satisfactory or utterly disturbing, often both at the same time. Nevertheless, this combination enables very deep, authentic and long-lasting relationships.

The German novelist and Nobel prize winner **Thomas Mann** (1875 – 1955) had a chart with Neptune in the 8th as ruler of the 7th, trine Mars in Capricorn in the 4th. His resolute and ingenious wife Katja made it possible that the father of six children could always work in peace and was kept from everyday profanities. The moody and complex novelist (*The Magic Mountain*), hid his homosexual tendencies and was particularly ambivalent towards his three sons, two of whom were gay and two committed suicide.

French chef **Paul Bocuse** (1926 – 2008) had Uranus in the 8th as ruler of a crowded 7th house, trine Saturn in the 4th, quincunx Neptune in the 1st house and square Mars in Capricorn in the 5th house. Bocuse came to fame on account of his high-quality restaurants and innovative cooking, being one of the most prominent chefs of nouvelle cuisine.

Ruler of 8th in 7th

This constellation, a bit like the 4th in the 7th house or the 12th in the 7th house, brings a lot of emotional baggage into encounters with other people or the public at large. This can be very subliminal and subconscious, but never a matter of indifference. These natives can be truly fascinating. On the other hand, there is a strong risk of projecting their own neurotic issues onto others, which can feel rather daunting. There is a certain element of breaking taboos and overstepping boundaries as well, which might feel either exciting or intimidating, often both at the same time. Any partner carries, so to speak, the key to our Pandora's Box and could unleash our jealously, envy, anger and possessiveness any time. The task is to grow spiritually with each and every encounter and try to find a way of treating others with respect and trust instead of having to constantly fight in underhand power games.

In the chart of **RuPaul Charles,** the famous American drag performer, born 1960, we find Saturn in Capricorn in the 7th as ruler of the 8th, opposition Mars/Lilith in Cancer, sextile Moon in Scorpio in the 5th house. The flamboyant RuPaul, after years of hardship, is enjoying a very successful career (*RuPaul's Drag Race*) and is also married to down-to-earth rancher Georges LeBar; they spend their time in the countryside. He is famous for quotes like "If you can't love yourself, then how the hell can you love somebody else?"

Pierre Casiraghi, born 1987, son of Princess Caroline of Monaco, has Uranus in the 6th as ruler of 8th house, trine Jupiter in Aries in the 10th, square Mercury and Venus in the 3rd and opposition Chiron in the 12th. He was three years old when his father, speedboat racer Stefano, was killed in a boat accident. He himself is a passionate boat and car racer, and, although at one time dismissed as a playboy, is also seriously involved in a multitude of charities. He accompanied Greta Thunberg on her sea trip to the USA in 2019.

Ruler of 8th in 8th
This placement often comes with the drive to penetrate to the core of things, come what may. Intensity is the flavour of life. Others, however mesmerised by the charisma, can nevertheless feel overwhelmed. Emotions,

normally under control, can erupt and shock everyone else. Constantly wanting to feel danger, lust, control and play power games means walking on thin ice. Compromise is not in their repertoire either, since it feels too much like defeat and weakness. It is therefore crucial to find something in life to dedicate oneself to, if possible, in a constructive way. After surviving many challenges, one can find a deep inner satisfaction, like in no other constellation. Sexuality, finances, crises, psychology, crime and any sort of boundary crossing might serve as a field of activity.

Evel Knievel (1938 – 2007), American stunt performer and entertainer, had Mercury in Libra, as ruler of the 8th in the 8th house, in a square with Pluto. The fearless daredevil performed ramp-to-ramp motorcycle jumps more than 75 times. Over the time he had broken 35 bones and had 14 surgeries, but always claimed that he could overcome pain and go on, no matter what.

Socialite and hotel heiress **Paris Hilton**, born 1981, has a Leo Moon on the North Node in the 8th as ruler of the 8th house quincunx Mars in Pisces in the 3rd, opposite Venus in Aquarius in the 2nd and trine Uranus in the 12th. 'It girl' Hilton has always enjoyed to party and flirt. Being a bit of an exhibitionist, her motto is 'No matter what a woman looks like, if she is confident, she's sexy.' In 2004, however, she was exposed worldwide in a sex tape with her then-boyfriend Rick Fallomon, which left her feeling deeply humiliated.

Ruler of 8th in 9th

Both houses deal with discovery, albeit with a totally different focus. In the 9th house our wings spread out and we want to take off, up, up and away. In the 8th the journey takes us down into the catacombs of our psyche. If the ruler of the 8th is in the 9th we might learn about our hidden agendas by encountering foreign countries, learning another language or seeking spiritual inspiration in religion. Also learning becomes crucial, often in a lifelong effort to satisfy one's enormous curiosity. This sounds fun and entertaining, but it is not really. As a matter of fact, it can be challenging and painful, leading to many a crisis. After all, at the end of the journey is nothing less than finding the Holy Grail. This journey might very well never be completed. We must not forget that the arrow which is shot by the centaur, the 9th house Sagittarian symbol, aims at a target way up in the sky, without a visible endpoint. This is a very fruitful combination for anyone who wants to teach out of deep inner conviction. On the other hand, it may also be tempting to interfere in other people's affairs.

Italian-American pop icon **Madonna Ciccone**, born 1958, has Mars in Taurus in the 9th as ruler of the 8th, in a trine with Moon in Virgo in the 1st and a square to Uranus in the 12th. A lot of her work deals with religious matters (*Like a Prayer*), which has often sparked controversy. Born and raised a Catholic, she later expanded her theological horizon by studying the Kabbalah and trying to follow religious practices affiliated with Judaism.

The French ecclesiastic and politician **Cardinal Richelieu** (1585 – 1642) had a Leo Venus in the 9th as ruler of the 8th house in a quincunx aspect with Uranus in the 4th house and a square with Mars in Scorpio in the 1st house. Richelieu is one of history's great Machiavellian figures, who lived by the mantra 'the ends justify the means'. He had great influence over the weak-willed King Louis XIII and was a key figure in the Thirty Years' War, in which he, albeit being a staunch Roman Catholic, often supported the German Protestants against the Catholic Hapsburg monarchy in order to increase the standing of France as a European power to be reckoned with. He was allegedly the most feared and hated man in France.

Ruler of 9th in 8th

This combination can be even more exciting than 8th in 9th. The native is confronted with his or her shadow by travelling, broadening their horizon and matters of faith. And since any fascinating encounter with the wider world could inspire profound self-discovery, there is always the danger of overstimulation. Therefore, it is crucial to develop a filter system in order to distance oneself every now and then, maybe more often than other people. Periods of withdrawal are important to process those intense experiences and can sometimes have a cleansing, almost cathartic effect. But there is also a darker side to this placement, for sometimes one might feel overwhelmed and plunged into feelings of anger, fear and sadness, almost like a déjà vu experience.

In the chart of **King George IV** (1762 – 1830), Mars in Scorpio rules the 9th and is placed in the 8th. It is part of a T-square with opposition Moon/Jupiter in Taurus and square Sun/Neptune on the descendant. Mars is also challenged by a quincunx with Uranus. The eldest son of the strict and difficult George III, who later in life became mentally ill, had a very frugal and loveless childhood. He later became very obese and had a hunger for sex, art, fashion, food and drink. His reign fell into the glamorous Regency period, named after him. The exotic palace in Brighton, Indian from outside, Chinese from inside reflects perfectly an eccentric 9th house taste.

The American astrologer **Chris Brennan,** born 1984, has a Scorpio Pluto in the 8th as ruler of the 9th house, in conjunction with the Sun and trine the Moon in Aquarius in the 1st house. He specialises in Hellenistic astrology, which is based on Greco-Roman traditions. Brennan is an ardent advocate for using these ancient methods in modern, everyday use of astrology.

Ruler of 8th in 10th

This combination involves some of the positive aspects of Mars in Capricorn, the red planet's position of exaltation. It often brings dedication and goal-orientation. One is focused on social status, responsibility and the goals in life. At some crucial point in their life many people get in touch with some kind of calling. This is often only felt after having fought several crises. And although this requires overcoming one's fears and apprehensiveness, taking on a certain direction seems unavoidable. This placement can often have the effect that the native either actively wants to take charge or that others want him subliminally to take the lead. At the same time, one might easily clash with authority figures who don't like to subordinate themselves.

American outlaw, robber, guerrilla and gang leader **Jesse James** (1847 – 1882) had a retrograde Saturn in Pisces on his MC as ruler of the 8th house, opposing the Sun in the 2nd, trine Jupiter in the 1st and sextile Mars in the 11th. Despite being a notoriously ruthless criminal and killer, he was idolised as a sort of modern day Robin Hood.

American film producer **Cecil B. De Mille** (1881 – 1959) had a crowded 10th house with Mars, Jupiter, Saturn, Chiron, Neptune and Pluto. Neptune is the ruler of the 8th house conjunct Chiron, Jupiter and Saturn, square the Sun on the Leo ascendant and trine Uranus in the 2nd house. De Mille was famous for his lavish productions like *The Greatest Show on Earth* and *The Ten Commandments*. He was the first director to combine art with film-making and created the title of 'art director' in film.

Ruler of 10th in 8th

This placement allows for several scenarios. The goal in life could be to constantly challenge oneself and go through deep transformations. After times of stagnancy a crisis might lead to questioning the pursued path and rethinking it. There is always the quest for something or someone passionate and authentically thrilling. On the other hand, it might take a long time to overcome one's own self-criticism and apprehensiveness to really recognise one's real urges and visions. Everything involving psychology, crime, death or the values of others might be tempting here, as well as boundary crossing of any sort.

American industrialist and founder of Standard Oil **John D. Rockefeller Senior** (1839 – 1937) had Saturn in Sagittarius as ruler of the 10th house in the 8th, trine Mars/Jupiter in the 6th, square Venus in the 5th and trine Mercury in the 4th. He adhered to total abstinence.

Konrad Adenauer (1876 – 1967) was the first chancellor of the Federal Republic of Germany after WWII. He used his influence to see that West Germany joined the side of western capitalist countries in the Cold War and join NATO. The oldest head of government ever, he belied his age by his passion for work and uncanny political instinct. In his chart Jupiter in Scorpio is ruler of the 10th, trine Mars in Pisces in the 1st and interwoven in a grand cross with Uranus in the 5th, Pluto in the 2nd and Saturn in Aquarius in the 12th.

Ruler of 8th in 11th

This placement often inclines to seek intensive friendships with kindred spirits in order to be challenged and to challenge others. Small talk doesn't come easy and superficial encounters are experienced as extremely tiring and draining. There is also a need to connect with those who at first glance appear to be moody, aloof or overly dramatic. All in all, there is a tendency to either fall for people completely or not feel any interest whatsoever. There needs to be a careful selection process. Since the 11th house also encompasses aspirations, contributions, altruism and ideals, there is an absolute necessity to find inspiring groups, however small or odd they might appear. The 11th and 8th houses, both of fixed modality, form a natural square. Water and air can easily clash because passion and emotions might come in the way of cool rational intellect. It might be for example that we find ourselves in the role of agent provocateur in a group of people, giving them a hard time, quite unintentionally. It could also be that we act as a catalyst in order to bring people to self-confrontation and transformation.

Ruth Ellis (1926 – 1955) was the last woman in England to be executed, which led to mass protests and eventually the abolishment of the death penalty for women. In her chart the retrograde Jupiter in Aquarius is ruler of the 8th house and part of a grand cross with Mars in the 12th, Neptune in the 5th and Moon/Saturn in Scorpio in the 7th. The platinum blonde single mother was working in fashionable Knightsbridge as a nightclub hostess when she met David Blakely, a posh former public-school boy and hard-drinking racer. They began a tempestuous affair which ended by her shooting him out of jealousy.

English karmic astrologer **Judy Hall** (1943 - 2021) had Uranus in Gemini in the 11th as ruler of the 8th house, in opposition with Sun/Mercury in Sagittarius in the 5th and a trine with Neptune in the 3rd house. Hall had a more intuitive way of working with the horoscope, which she herself described as divination. One of her works is *Karmic Connections*.

Ruler of 11th in 8th

This combination brings hopes, friends and groups right to the centre of our own hidden psychological issues. This is a very passionate placement, because our experiences often cause transformations. We might feel challenged and provoked by society, but we take up the gauntlet. People might find us very fascinating and project a lot of their subconscious passion on to us. Friendships can have a catalyst effect, but we might also be tempted to play with the persona that others see in us, rather than dare to show our real self. Financial issues might play an important role as well when dealing with like-minded groups. Another possibility is to find ourselves in entanglements which are difficult to untangle. On the other hand, there is a great capacity for zest of life and long-lasting relationships and commitments.

Actor **Ryan O'Neal**, born 1941, has an Aquarius Mars as ruler of the 11th in his 8th house, square Saturn in Taurus in the 11th and sextile Mercury in Aries in the 10th. Since Uranus, the ruler of the 8th, is in his 11th house, this connection is very intense. The former sex symbol and movie star (*Love Story*), who always had troubles with romantic commitments, had a passionate relationship with actress Farrah Fawcett (*Charlie's Angels*). They remained friends and saw each other through tough times; both were at one time battling with cancer, of which Fawcett finally died.

President **John F. Kennedy** (1917 – 1963) had a very full 8th house in his chart with Sun, Mercury, Venus, Mars and Jupiter. His Gemini Sun is the ruler of the 11th house in the 8th, conjunct Venus, trine Neptune in the 10th and square Moon in Virgo in the 11th. The 11th house is about hopes and society's development. The charismatic Kennedy was the projection figure for hope and change for a whole generation. Looking deeper into his 8th house, we actually now know more about his darker sides. He might not have won the 1960 elections without the massive funds of his millionaire father and the help of the mafia. He was sexually insatiable and suffered from various ailments, the treatment for which made him a drug addict.

Ruler of 8th in 12th

Both are water houses and involved with the exchange of emotional and unconscious issues. This placement is very difficult to pin down, since the 12th house is a place of secrets and disguise. The motive of the ruler of the 8th house is always to find authenticity and to find one's own true essence. In the 12th this process might require long periods of withdrawal.

Privacy is often very important for these natives. Since the 8th house also encompasses intimate relationships, the partner often plays a key role. If the relationship is a constructive, supportive one, crises only intensify mutual feelings of love and trust, and matters of the 12th house present themselves from a joyous perspective. The keyword is devotion. This might also apply to a cause or a vision. On the other hand, if relationships are of a more destructive nature, there is a danger of getting lost in addictions, deceptions or becoming a victim. One might experience self-conquest 'behind the scenes', in institutions or yoga retreats. Also, nature and music can have a positive influence. There also might be underhanded dealing when it comes to financial resources or money might simply disappear.

Former Prime Minister **Tony Blair**, born 1953, has a Taurus Jupiter at the critical degree of 29° in the 12th as ruler of the 7th and the 8th house, in conjunction with Mars in Gemini on the ascendant. Blair was the main source behind the New Labour movement which finally swept him into office in 1997. While he was charismatic and compelling at his most popular times, he later fell from grace over supporting George W. Bush in the Iraq war without UN backing. His wife Cherie, with whom he has four children, is a self-confident figure and believed to have a strong influence over Blair. To this day, despite the attempts of many experts and former companions to pigeon-hole him, Blair remains very much an enigma.

Former Spice Girl and wife of football star David, **Victoria Beckham**, born 1974, has Saturn at 29° Gemini as ruler of the 8th house in the 12th. This conjunction forms the apex of a grand trine with Moon in Aquarius in the 9th and Uranus in Libra in the 5th. It is also the apex of a T-square with Pluto in the 4th and Mercury in the 10th. Beckham is known to be a very ambitious and controlling businesswoman, wife and mother of four children. She seldom smiles and has created an impeccably dressed public persona, very fitting for the 12th house. While her chart has no earth, except Black Moon Lilith in Capricorn in the 7th, her husband David, who also has the ruler of the 8th in the 12th house, has quite a lot of earth in his chart.

Ruler of 12th in 8th

This combination can bring on a subtle, unconditional yearning to entirely merge oneself into a relationship, a vision or a cause, although it might be disappointed by unrealistic, over-idolised expectations. However, it enables the native to instinctively get right to the heart of an issue, be it financially, therapeutically or sexually, thus bearing the potential for cathartic experiences and psychologically cleansing effects.

Prince Philip Mountbatten (1921 - 2021) had a Virgo Jupiter as ruler of the 11th and the 12th in the 8th house conjunct Saturn, in opposition with Uranus in the 2nd, sextile Pluto in the 6th and Venus on the IC. His story is that of a male Cinderella. The son of a discharged impoverished and philandering Greco-German prince, he experienced an unstable childhood. When his third cousin, Princess Elizabeth fell in love with him at age 13, his fate was sealed. He had to renounce his own foreign title as a Greek prince and become a British citizen. But being married to one of the wealthiest women on earth came with a price. He had to give up his career in the navy and was restricted to merely ceremonial duties and charity work. Being independent, ambitious and hot-tempered by nature, one can only conclude that his love for his wife was genuine. His loyalty, certainly, was remarkable.

Another example of someone who is dedicated to a cause is the British politician **Nigel Farage**, born 1964. In his chart we find the Sun in Aries as ruler of the 12th house in conjunction with Mars and in quincunx to Pluto on his Virgo ascendant. He is the former leader of the UK Independence Party (UKIP) and since 2019 leader of his own Brexit party. Farage, as a polarising public figure, to say the least, has many followers and definitely has a talent to convince people. He has been a staunch critic of the European Union and seems to have only one goal: for the UK to leave the bloc. This is possibly an interesting stance for a man with Huguenot and German ancestors.

9
Transits Through the 8th House

Mars

Mars is the traditional ruler of Scorpio and also the collective ruler of the 8th house. This is familiar territory, so the more persistent, penetrating qualities of the red planet can come to the fore. It is, nevertheless, a malefic in traditional astrology, feared to bring bad luck and misfortune. What it usually does bring on is a time in which one feels an increase in activity on various levels. There may also be more friction than usual, forcing us to come out of our corner to fight. Whether this is more in a defensive or offensive way depends on the main character of the native. Mars can fight for something just as well as fighting against something. We can feel attacked by others and want to snap back. In many cases staying cool, calm and collected is no longer an option. Also playing fair and expecting good manners from others is not on the menu right now. How we deal with the challenges of this time depends largely on how we generally own our Mars in our chart.

This can also be a time of increased sexual excitability; maybe we are tempted to explore taboos? Mars could bring some adventure in our love life and help us to let off some steam.

Suppressed emotions might pop up now, both inside ourselves and in those around us. Conflicts can play around sexual, financial and other power issues. We might feel a bit off balance and need to see life on an even keel again. This can be quite difficult, because this time often makes us impatient, unjust and touchy. Also guilt issues can become pressing, either in a financial or moral context. Do we owe someone? Or does someone owe us? Now fate demands clarity. Do we fight? Do we face the facts? Or do we rather procrastinate and leave business unfinished for the time being?

However one decides to handle this powerful energy, it can never be done by halves. There will always be the element of provocation and boundary crossing. After all, you cannot bake a cake without breaking eggs. Relationships will often be put to the test also. And while some will flourish, others will perish. We now have to fight our little battles in life and we need to be responsible, because any actions will have an impact on how we deal with our partner in the future.

Jupiter

Jupiter in transit usually brings light-heartedness and optimism in every house and it also holds true for the 8th house of crises. The universe might grant us a generous credit now. And although this might not necessarily affect our finances, it can be a great time to live off other people's gratitude and affection.

New and exciting energy vibes might emerge in our relationships, so this is a good time to embrace the chance to open up and trust our partners. Suppressed fears and anger may now dissolve, maybe supported by a therapist. The main thing is to really make the best of this transit before it travels on to the 9th house, where Jupiter will shine and widen our horizons. Cleansing, making amends and embracing our weaknesses and shadows are on the homework list now. Why not push some boundaries too? You are braver and more courageous than you think.

Saturn

During its transit, Saturn, the big examiner, is the biggest expert when it comes to shedding light on our hidden weaknesses and shortcomings. For the 8th house, this means that we really have to pay up. Sometimes we have to literally part with financial resources or need to take up a credit. Our partnerships might involve us now in unexpectedly burdensome entanglements. We might have to put in a lot more energy to support people who are near and dear to us. Frustrating. But at the end of this transit we often feel so much more mature and complete in our journey of self-conquest. This is no time for idleness and dreaming. As a matter of fact, we might have to face a good deal of checking, re-evaluation and disillusionment. The glow has worn off and life feels much more serious now. Saturn reveals where we have failed so far and demands that we do our homework again. Often, issues from about 14 years before when it was visiting our 2nd house come up again, so we might need to check on them and maybe start everything afresh. On the other hand, if our relationships and projects are on solid ground and well-thought through, we will only become more self-confident.

Our relationships might feel a lot more serious at the moment. Time to face the truth: do we still want to invest in them and nourish them or is it maybe time for a clean break? The bottom line is, the honeymoon is over and we need to embrace the shortcomings in ourselves and our partner. And if you flip the coin, this need for re-evaluation also holds true, vice versa. Maybe our partner is disappointed by us? The challenge now is not to shy away from facing honest and constructive discussion.

Also, any sort of financial draining might push us to our very limits. Even coming into money might feel like a double-edged sword, bringing on more responsibility than freedom. It is hardly a time to come into money without there being any strings attached. The 8th is also the house of subconscious projections. We often need to project because we don't want to feel the painful burden of negative emotions and don't want to see ourselves as we really are. Now these projections can come back to us and haunt us. Any identity crisis now presents us with a profound chance to come to terms with our shadows.

Chiron

Chiron deals with our wounds, scars and innermost shame. It is all about a deeply hidden yearning for compassion, comfort and healing. Its visit in the 8th house can open the floodgates unexpectedly and we might feel particularly vulnerable. At the same time, we can connect with others intimately; the perfect time for licking each other's wounds. But this requires courage. So often in life we try to hide our sensitivity. Let's use this transit to embrace our Achilles heel. At the end of the day it is always best to own the full range of all your emotions, be it joyous or painful, because in the 8th house you cannot have one without the other. This can be the chance to forgive yourself for long-forgotten mistakes and make peace with regrets. Shame and guilt issues will probably pop up and require your whole capacity for self-healing. And although you might not feel up to it, it is a good time to let others come closer to you. Being near to someone who can feel your pain and vice versa can now be a new source of real intimacy.

Uranus

Uranus can be both liberating and disruptive. During its journey through the houses it usually initiates a certain need to break free. We might feel the urge to be less conventional in matters of this house. When analysing its transits through the houses it is however more important to look at medium- and long-term effects. Uranus, while being in a house, might turn everything topsy-turvy. In the 8th house Uranus wants to free hidden agendas, suppressed emotions and entanglements. This process might be actively supported by the native or fought against. In the latter case life can feel pretty unsettling during this time. It also seems to depend upon how we have dealt with our 8th house before. In any case, Uranus often presents us with surprises. Things might take unexpected turns and people might notice facets in our behaviour which had been hidden before. Finances might be a bit wobbly during the transit. Uranian disruptions often occur spasmodically. If the native has a lot of air in his or her chart or a dominant

Uranus, this might feel utterly liberating and joyous. If, on the other hand, we have a lot of earth and water or fixed modality in the chart, it might feel threatening, as if someone has pulled the rug out from underneath you. If relationships are too symbiotic and suffocating, it's best to go back a step and try out how it feels with a little bit more distance. This isn't necessarily about breaking up, but rather to experience the boundaries. Being more independent and giving each other more freedom does not mean to become totally non-committed.

Neptune

Neptune can stay in a house for ten or more years, so its impact is long-lasting. Neptune often deals with dissolution. It also encompasses both idealisation and de-idealisation. It invites us to dream, which is pleasurable. But at the same time, it can also confuse us with deceptions, which often have less pleasurable consequences. Does this sound contradictory or confusing? Well, welcome to Neptune's world! This can be indeed a time when we find it hard to judge whether things in our life are true or not. Neptune might dissolve anything, which isn't strictly true or realistic. Maybe it is about time to realise that we have lost our way and need to find the way back. Since the 8th house deals with relationships, money, sexuality and unfinished business, it is necessary to disentangle any sort of muddle. What Neptune wants us to face, oddly enough, is where we have been deceived or are deceiving others or ourselves. What kind of issues will be activated when other natal planets are hit by transit during this period? Another issue might be atonement and forgiveness to be able to find peace again. This is a good time to embrace spirituality or undergo any sort of therapy.

Pluto

Pluto transits are the slowest, so its effect can be felt for many years. This holds even truer for its visit in a house. According to the size of the house this visit can activate the issues of this house sometimes for a whole decade or more. Pluto, similar to Neptune, works in a very subtle but nevertheless intense and long-lasting way. The 8th house is its natural habitat; issues like crises and transformation come naturally to the ruler of the underworld. Power struggles and the need for self-conquest deliver the subtext over this long period. Something or someone has to die, be it an image which is not valid anymore, a relationship, or indeed a person. This mourning process requires emotional and mental skills, which are the hardest to learn in life, since they don't come with a manual. We all have to battle a loss in our own way. To seek help therefore, is not a sign of weakness but rather of strength. Suppressed memories can pop up any time and lead to all sorts of feelings. Anger, sadness, rancour, envy and other unpleasant emotions can form a kind of subconscious pressure. To deal constructively with these emotions might seem impossible, but that is not the case. The first step, like in any kind of therapy, is always to accept feelings. Do we feel any sort of manipulation going on? Do we understand its patterns? How did they form in the past? Of course, Pluto will be felt more precisely when it activates a planet in the 8th house or forms an aspect to planets during its time in this house. Typically, one often only feels the purpose of this transit after Pluto has travelled on to the 9th house.

Epilogue

It's always an adventure to write a book, and there are many ups and downs in store along the way. Anyone who claims that "the words simply pour out" is lying, I dare say. Writing is hard work. It is so in your own language and it's even more daunting in another language. I adore the English language, always have and always will. I lived in London for a time and will always treasure the memories; it is my home away from home, Brexit or no Brexit. When I began to write articles for German and Austrian magazines I thought, why not write something in English for a change? Which is what I did. And when I handed in two articles for the Astrological Association Journal I was thrilled to be accepted. That gave me a big boost. I was also encouraged by my lectures for the Astrological Lodge, AFAN, NORWAC, the AA conference and MISPA, which made me more self-confident. I felt more and more at ease and even started to really enjoy myself. I have a full 9th house with Mercury at the apex of a Yod as chart ruler, since I have Virgo rising. This means that although I am all for expanding my horizons, learning, teaching and exploring other languages (9th house), I am also uber-critical and tend to feel that I am not good enough (Virgo rising).

When I approached Margaret Cahill from The Wessex Astrologer with the idea of translating my German book on the 8th house, she was immediately hooked. Right, I thought, then let's get to it. But translating a book is not as easy as I thought. I struggled with finding the right tone, words, meaning, etc. A story may not necessarily come across as well in English as it does in German. After all, English differs dramatically from German. In English, a word can have many different meanings according to the context. In contrast, in German there is a word for everything; we Germans really seem to want to express ourselves precisely, without any risk of being misunderstood. To cut a long story short, at one point I grew tired of the monotonous translation. Then it dawned on me that I needed a change, so I decided that instead of just translating the book, chapter after chapter, I would leave out certain chapters and swap them for new ones instead. So, by writing parts from scratch, I wasn't so hindered by difficult translation challenges. It was much easier to write directly in English. By creating parts of the book afresh, I felt invigorated. It gave me a chance to alter the book according to what I felt, two years after the German version, that I wanted to add or modify. In the end, I left out the stories about:

- RAF (Rote Armee Fraktion): a terrorist group which held West Germany in fear during the dramatic year of 1977.
- Vera Brühne: a beautiful and infamously independent woman who, in 1962, was charged with a life-long prison sentence for a double homicide which she most probably didn't commit.
- Günther Wallraff: an investigative journalist who shocked Germany by exploiting scandals about racism, press manipulation, food poisoning and several other cases.
- Mata Hari: the glamorous WW1 spy who, as it turned out wasn't much good at what she did. Her story is much more a vivid example of being entangled in narcissistic illusions.
- Lord Byron: the promiscuous poet star who couldn't find love and was chased by his traumatic childhood.

Instead, I put in stories about:
- Kaiser Wilhelm and his mother Vicky
- Truman Capote and Perry Smith
- Princess Beatrice and Queen Victoria
- Jane Goodall
- Tab Hunter

I also considerably enriched the final chapters about placements in the 8th house by adding many more examples and by including the nodes and Black Moon Lilith.

My shadow is pink

The 8th house is all about coming to terms with our own shadow(s). Well, it so happens that I was given a very lovely children's book by my partner the other day, called *My Shadow is Pink* by Scott Stuart. It is about a boy who likes all things girlie: dolls, dresses, ponies etc. On his first day of school all the kids are encouraged to dress in their favourite outfits. In his case, this is a yellow dress. His father wants to dissuade him from this, fearing that he will be laughed at. When the boy enters the classroom he immediately senses that he is different from the other boys, who all look at him in amazement. He runs home, seeking comfort from his father who explains to his son that every person has a hidden side with secret yearnings about being someone else - out of the box, not fitting in. The next day his dad puts on a dress himself and goes to school with the boy, where he meets his first friend.

This is a very touching story. To me personally in particular, because it reminded me of my own childhood and struggles with traditional gender roles. When I was a boy, there was nothing I wanted more than to become a ballet dancer. Alas, it was not to be, as the adults thought it would be inappropriate. I am not saying that kids are totally free from gender stereotypes these days; far from it. The world seems ever more divided into pink versus blue. And still, stories like that or TV formats like *RuPaul's Drag Race* serve as a platform for so many kids and (young) people who feel that they don't fit in and that there is something wrong with them. But at the end of the day, we all have to struggle with taboos and facets of ourselves which are hidden in the shadow. The task is to embrace this shadow, own it and bring it out into the light.

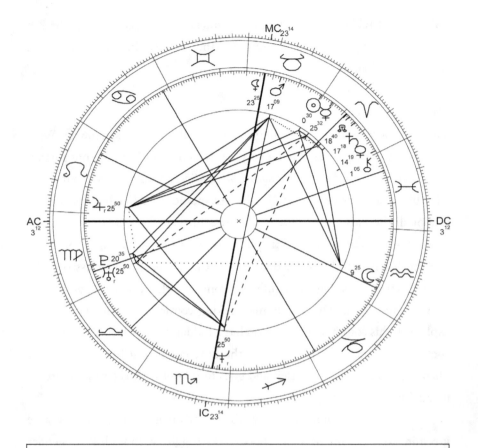

Martin Sebastian Moritz, 20 April 1968, 13:48 UT, Hamburg, Germany

8th house constellations

- Venus, Saturn, Chiron and North Node in Aries in 8th
- Neptune, ruler of 8th at IC as part of a yod with Mercury and Uranus
- Venus in 8th as ruler of 3rd and 10th
- Saturn in 8th as ruler of 5th
- Venus conjunction Saturn in sextile with Moon in Aquarius in 6th

Index

ABOUT THE AUTHOR

Martin Sebastian Moritz lives in Hamburg and Berlin. He started out as actor and dancer before his life took a different turn and he decided to study psychology and astrology. With ten years of teaching psychodrama under his belt, he now specialises in couples therapy, often supported by astrological readings, and has been a consulting psychological astrologer for more than two decades. Martin lectures all over Germany, Austria, Switzerland and the UK and has given talks at NORWAC, the AA conference and the London-based Astrological Lodge. He also lectures for MISPA. He writes articles for German and Swiss astrology magazines, as well as for the Astrological Journal. He specialises in psychological and karmic astrology, and gender issues, and uses astrology as a tool to better understand couple dynamics, life challenges and mundane patterns in history. An Anglophile, for a while he lived in London, his home away from home. *Pandora's Box: The Mysterious 8th House* was originally published in German as *Das rätselhafte 8. Haus: Der Schatten im Horoskop*. His website is astro-via.com.

CPSIA information can be obtained
at www.ICGtesting.com
Printed in the USA
LVHW031159120522
718584LV00004B/70